LOBSTERS
SCREAM
WHEN YOU
BOIL THEM

LOBSTERS SCREAM WHEN YOU BOIL THEM

And 100 Other Myths About Food and Cooking . . .

Plus 25 Recipes to Get It Right Every Time

Bruce Weinstein and **Mark Scarbrough**

WITHDRAWN

G
GALLERY
BOOKS

NEW YORK LONDON TORONTO SYDNEY

Gallery Books
A Division of Simon & Schuster, Inc.
1230 Avenue of the Americas
New York, NY 10020

First Gallery Books trade paperback edition July 2011

GALLERY BOOKS and colophon are registered trademarks of
Simon & Schuster, Inc.

For information about special discounts for bulk purchases,
please contact Simon & Schuster Special Sales at 1-866-506-1949
or business@simonandschuster.com.

The Simon & Schuster Speakers Bureau can bring authors to your
live event. For more information or to book an event contact the
Simon & Schuster Speakers Bureau at 1-866-248-3049 or visit
our website at www.simonspeakers.com.

Designed by Level C

Manufactured in the United States of America

10 9 8 7 6 5 4 3 2 1

Library of Congress Cataloging-in-Publication Data

Weinstein, Bruce.
    Lobsters scream when you boil them : and 100 other myths about food and
cooking : plus 25 recipes to get it right every time / by Bruce Weinstein
and Mark Scarbrough.—1st Gallery Books trade paperback ed.
        p. cm.
    1. Food. 2. Nutrition—Popular works. 3. Cooking. I. Scarbrough, Mark.
II. Title.
    TX355.W425 2011
    641.3—dc22
2011011095

ISBN 978-1-4391-9537-6
ISBN 978-1-4391-9538-3 (ebook)

CONTENTS

IN THE BEGINNING . . .

Bruce and I have had a set plan for writing our previous twenty books: we dream up the recipes together, he goes into the kitchen, we taste them, we argue, some are perfect, some go back to the drawing board, and I eventually write the book.

This one's different. We *wrote* it together. He ensconced himself in an overstuffed chair beside my desk and we went at it.

But the *idea* for the book started with a phone call.

"What's the thing about the butter?"

My mother and I dispensed with *hello* years ago. For people whose progenitors fell during the Siege of Chattanooga, we're downright gruff. Like New Yorkers with heirloom silver.

"The butter?" I sighed.

"I'm baking cookies."

"Are you using one of our recipes?"

She's a diminutive Southerner who's never cooked one of the more than ten thousand recipes Bruce and I have developed.

"You know I love you, dear."

I didn't take the bait. "Mother, we've been over this butter thing before."

"I know. But what's the good of having a son go to grad school, marry a prominent executive, get divorced, come out, move to New York, write screenplays, marry a chef, and do cookbooks with him, all if *I* have to remember this stuff? Can't I just call you up?"

"At eight thirty in the morning?"

"You're so busy."

"I live in rural New England!"

"Let me have my imagination. So the butter?"

"Cool. Almost right out of the fridge."

"Not room temperature?" she asked. "Are you sure? My cookbook says *room temperature.*"

"When was it published?"

"Don't get sarcastic. I warned you this would happen if you went to a liberal arts college."

"The butter has to be cool to trap air and make a better batter. Preferably just moments out of the fridge."

"Now that wasn't so hard, was it?"

Easy for her to say. Like the rest of us, she's surrounded by culinary ripsnorters. We read them in magazines, hear them on cooking shows. Who can keep the facts straight?

Eggs raise your cholesterol.

Gas stoves are superior to electric.

Your tongue has four kinds of taste buds.

They seem benign, right? What could it matter if people think that sugar makes them hyper or that margarine is better for them than butter?

It matters because these whoppers warp recipes. Here's a headnote we recently found: "These cookies are better for your kids because they have almost no sugar. You're saving yourself hours of screaming and running around the house."

Too bad the cookies are also tasteless. You're clearly saving yourself the trouble of eating them, too.

Some myths get passed off as down-from-the-mount truths. Like *Never salt steaks before you cook them.* But then you miss the best part: the caramelized sugars, extracted from the surface of the beef over the heat by the dehydrating action of the salt, all to give that steak an irresistible, sweet-salty-savory crunch on the outside, even when the meat's rare inside.

Other myths aren't just wrongheaded; they lead to kitchen failures. Like *Peanut oil is tasteless.* Then someone has a craving for sweets, has no other oil in the house, substitutes peanut oil willy-nilly for the fat in a recipe of white chocolate brownies, and ends up with a big pan of *blech.*

Not many of these doozies are outright lies. Almost all are based on a half-stated fact or a small misunderstanding that got larded up over the years.

Turkey makes you sleepy.

Spicy foods cool you down.

A box of baking soda in the refrigerator absorbs odors.

No, no, and no.

We'll delve into the whys and wherefores that debunk 101 of the most common kitchen myths, so you can get it right every time. If you want more research, footnotes, scholarly articles, and such, we've got a full list of links to them on our website, www.realfoodhascurves.com.

Mom, are you reading?

Of course not.

1

BECAUSE WE'VE ALWAYS DONE IT THAT WAY

The Ten Classics

Repeat a lie enough and it starts to sound like the truth. Publish it enough and it starts to become the truth.

After years of reading cookbooks and food articles, we've seen our share of unsubstantiated food mythology pass into the realm of received wisdom. We've done our best to set the record straight, but spreading the word at Q & A sessions after cooking demonstrations has felt a lot like lobbing pebbles at Cossacks.

The following ten myths are the ones that we have identified as the most pervasive forms of erroneous common knowledge. Call these the culinary equivalents of "blondes have more fun."

FOR BAKING, THE BUTTER SHOULD BE AT ROOM TEMPERATURE.

ALMOST NEVER.

Ever read a cookie or cake recipe that calls for *unsalted butter, at room temperature*? Too bad such advice leads to flatter cookies, denser cakes, and tough quick breads. Why? Natch, it goes back to chemistry.

Butter is an emulsion of fat and water, with some dairy solids in the mix. Emulsions are unstable by nature. Their parts do not fuse despite being homogenized. Instead, they remain separate in tiny droplets evenly distributed throughout.

A vinaigrette is an emulsion of oil and vinegar with some herbs thrown in for good measure. The fizzy foam on a cup of espresso is another emulsion—this time, of coffee oils and water. Both lead short lives. Oil and vinegar separate; the foam dissolves into the espresso.

So it is with butter. It can fall apart, particularly when warm. Just above 67°F, it starts to lose its coherence. Several degrees more and it becomes the soft spread that makes the desiccated hunk of bread we call *toast* edible.

As the temperature rises, butter continues to lose coherence. It soon spreads out, no longer able to hold even its basic shape—mostly because the solid fat in the emulsion is starting to liquefy. It used to hold the water in place; now it's letting go, loosening up, getting more Unitarian.

But below 67°F, the fat is stiffer, more Presbyterian. It can hold its water. And it can catch air. Hold it, too. Which is why you beat a batter in the first place: to trap air, particularly in the fat.

Thus, in most cases cool butter builds better batters. Cookies won't be flat; cakes will rise properly. Even cinnamon rolls will be more irresistible. (Oh, great.)

Yes, there are some specialty recipes in which the butter must be at room temperature—for example, when you're laminating a dough to make croissants, repeatedly working the butter into the dough through incessant rolling. But these sorts of things are unusual, laborious, pastry-chef tasks. For most cakes, cookies, and quick breads, for anything where the *beaten* butter is to provide airy heft, cold butter is the way to go.

So how did this culinary zinger get started? Blame it on the '50s. Gone were the stand mixers, the behemoths our great-grandmothers hauled out to the counter. Every June Cleaver wanted a tidy hand mixer.

Unfortunately, this modern appliance couldn't handle chilled butter. Bits spun around the bowl like lottery balls. The motor was weaker, too; it burned out quickly. And so arose a misguided attempt at making baking easier on the gadgetry, but not necessarily better all-around—that is, the myth of room-temperature butter.

These days, we're back to the backbreaking stand mixers—they can handle the cool butter you've got in the fridge. Admittedly, that butter is a little too cold—the fat is way beyond Presbyterian, more like Dutch Reformed, probably around 40°F. Here's the problem: you need the butter cool enough to trap air but not so hard that it's petrified.

The solution? Drag the butter out of the chill, cut it into small bits, and drop them into the mixing bowl. By the time you've got the other ingredients out of the pantry, the butter bits will have warmed up just enough that they won't burn out the motor but will still grab the air and hang on tight.

Without a moment's hesitation, make that batter or dough! Because a better cookie is the whole reason anyone would ever want one of those honkin' big stand mixers that take up so much cabinet space.

CHOCOLATE CHUNK CINNAMON OAT COOKIES

Makes about 4 dozen cookies

Although salted butter outsells unsalted seven to one in the United States, unsalted butter is still the culinary standard. First off, the extra salt can lead to melting and boiling point differentials which may affect more temperamental recipes. But secondly, why should someone else determine the sodium content of your food? Yes, these crisp, flavorful cookies are better with a pinch of salt—but not the heavier pour in salted butter.

2 cups plus 2 tablespoons all-purpose flour
½ cup rolled oats (do not use quick-
cooking or steel-cut oats)
1 teaspoon baking soda
1 teaspoon ground cinnamon
1 teaspoon salt
16 tablespoons (2 sticks or ½ pound) cold,
unsalted butter, cut into small bits
1 cup packed light brown sugar
½ cup granulated white sugar
2 large eggs
1 tablespoon vanilla extract
1 pound bittersweet chocolate bars, broken
and cut into ¼-inch chunks
1 cup chopped walnuts

1. Position the rack in the center of the oven; preheat the oven to 375°F. Line a large baking sheet with parchment paper or a reusable silicone baking mat.

2. In a medium bowl, use a whisk or a fork to mix the flour, oats, baking soda, cinnamon, and salt. (Why? So the leavening and flavorings are evenly distributed in the dry ingredients.)

3. In a large bowl, beat the butter, brown sugar, and granulated sugar with an electric mixer at medium speed until fluffy, and until most of the sugar has dissolved, about 5 minutes. You'll need to scrape down the sides of the bowl occasionally with a rubber spatula. But don't be tempted to run that big mixer at a higher speed. More friction means more heat. Which means warmer butter.

4. Beat in the eggs one at a time, scraping down the inside of the bowl a few times and making sure the eggs are thoroughly incorporated in the batter. Beat in the vanilla.

5. Stop the beaters; pour in the flour mixture. Turn the beaters on low and mix in the flour, just until most of the white pockets have disappeared, not a moment more.

6. Turn off and remove the beaters; scrape any batter back into the bowl. Use a wooden spoon to stir in the chocolate and walnuts, thereby also fully incorporating the flour.

7. Roll heaping tablespoonfuls of the dough into balls between your palms. Set the balls on the prepared baking sheet, a couple of inches apart. Bake for 10 minutes.

8. Use a hot pad to pick up the baking sheet and give it a good rap against the baking rack. Continue baking for 2 minutes. Then do it again: a good rap against the baking rack. Continue baking until the cookies are brown and set, about 3 more minutes. Put the baking sheet on a wire rack and cool for 2 minutes, then use a thin spatula to transfer the cookies to the wire rack itself to continue cooling. Cool the baking sheet for 5 minutes before making another batch. Check to see if you need to replace the parchment paper because it's too fried from having dried out.

HOT SKILLET, COLD OIL.

ONLY ON RARE, CHEFFY OCCASIONS.

Ah, the '80s. It was a heady time in the American culinary scene. A bunch of wide-load Cajuns and a galloping gourmet lit a mania for food and cooking from Julia Child's smoldering spark. They did it with suspenders and shoulder pads. And this dead-wrong myth.

The oil in the skillet or pan must be hot, not "to seal in the juices" (we'll come back to that one), but to keep the meat or vegetables from sticking. Here's why:

- First, fat smoothes things out.

Believe it or not, the inside of your skillet or saucepan is not flat. It's landscaped with microscopic grooves, ridges, and gashes. Oil (or any melted fat, for that matter) fills these in. Likewise, cuts of meat or chopped vegetables are microscopically uneven. A thin layer of fat evens them out, too. So why do we care about smoothing things out? Because . . .

- Second, fat is a lubricant.

Now that the topography of your skillet is smoothed out, those many nicks and gashes don't snag your food. Thus, less sticking—which means less tearing, chipping, and even scorching.

• Finally, fat gets really hot.

Way beyond the boiling point of water. When food hits the hot oil, you get a good sizzle because the extraneous surface water on the meat or vegetable is instantly vaporized. The piece of food is then raised slightly above the skillet's hot surface, riding on a tiny layer of steam. Thus, the caramelizing sugars don't fuse to the surface below. And by the time all that vaporizing is over, the meat or vegetable has a dried-out, crunchy crust. You know, the best part of the meal. But that crust also serves a culinary purpose. Crunchy things usually don't stick together very well—if at all. It's also why patchouli-soaked hippie communes fail.

If you think about it: How could oil ever stay cool in a hot skillet? A tablespoon or two in a preheated 300°F to 500°F skillet instantly spreads out into a thin sheet and pops up to the skillet's surface temperature in milliseconds. There's no way you can work quickly enough for there to be a hot skillet with cool oil in it.

That said, sometimes you *want* cool oil in a skillet, particularly for very cheffy reasons. Like when you want to infuse the fat with herbs, or other flavors, so that the items to be sautéed pick up more sophisticated flavors. To pull this off, pour pantry-temperature oil into a cold skillet off the heat, add a star anise pod or slivered garlic cloves or Sichuan peppercorns or red pepper flakes or fresh rosemary spears, and set the contraption over medium-low heat.

As the oil comes up to a sizzle, those spices or herbs release their flavors into the fat for a more satisfying meal. When the oil is finally hot, remove the flavoring agents and you've got infused oil that'll crisp whatever you're cooking and impress even Cajun cooks as well as any gourmets who insist on galloping.

YOUR TONGUE HAS FOUR KINDS OF TASTE BUDS: SWEET, SALTY, SOUR, AND BITTER.

AND DO CHICKENS HAVE LIPS?

So much bad information gets bandied about in elementary school. Eating paste won't make you sick. Holding it in all day gives you character. And the darn tongue map: sweet on the tip, salty at the sides, sour farther back on the sides, and bitter way back in the center by the epiglottis.

Okay, debunking this myth is easy. Get up and go in the kitchen. We'll wait. Get a pinch of salt. Put it on the tip of your tongue, the part that's supposed to taste *sweet*. Do you taste salt? Yes.

Still don't buy it? Now get a pinch of sugar. Put it way back on the center of your tongue, on the alleged *bitter* receptors. Do you still taste sweet? Yes.

Done. And by the way, holding it in all day doesn't give you character.

So how'd this tenacious tongue myth get started? Back in 1901, a German professor, D. P. Hanig, conducted an "experiment" (we use the term loosely, as in "a state-funded science fair project") in which he asked people their subjective experience of taste. *Here ist ein apple. Vere do you taste eet on your tongue?*

He used no controls nor any critical apparatus to judge the answers he got. Maybe he had no time, what with Kaiser Wilhelm II driving the country into war. Still, Hanig blocked out the results of all that anecdotal evidence on the now-familiar map of the tongue. It soon got foisted got off onto children.

Here are the facts:

☞ By the 1970s, researchers believed there were differences in taste centers on the tongue; but they also thought these could move around, depending on a person's history, proclivities, and age.

☞ By the late 1980s, researchers had finally come to the conclusion that the actual differences between these tasting centers were, at best, minimal.

☞ Then in 2006, researchers actually found one of the many proteins that allow us to taste sour. And they found it all over the tongue, not just in one area.

Dr. Hanig did us no favors. The truth has been a long time coming, holding out at least until the late '80s, if not beyond, waiting for hard evidence like we got in 2006. And yet we continue to see that tongue map even these days. Why? Because of wineglass makers. They coo that the shape of their stemware directs the wine to the appropriate parts of the tongue. The wider Burgundy glass pours the wine onto the salty receptors and then back to the sour ones, letting us taste the savory notes, missing the overpowering sweet and bitter ones that would register in the tongue's center. It's a more pleasurable experience, they say. And a naughty wine.

Yeah, right. And they don't even have the Kaiser to pin that doozy on.

DECAFFEINATED COFFEE HAS NO CAFFEINE.

CLOSE BUT NO CIGAR!

It's midnight. You're wide awake. You paid the bills. You called your mother. Why can't you fall asleep? All you did was have a few cups of decaffeinated coffee.

Which contains caffeine. Based on U.S. standards, between two and twelve milligrams per cup. (Europeans have stricter standards, and so far less caffeine.)

It's not much, for sure. A cup of *regular* coffee has somewhere between a hundred and two hundred milligrams. But a few cups of decaf, combined with some sensitivity on your part, plus your usual anxiety levels—and bang, you're awake.

And don't be fooled by those big coffeehouse drinks, the frothed, whirred, whipped-cream-topped, Dairy-Queen-Blizzard-for-hipsters coffee drinks. Three or four shots of decaf espresso in that cup and you may have had as much caffeine as is in a can of Coke.

How do you get wired on caffeine?

It suppresses signaling mechanisms throughout your body: the unconscious stuff, the stuff that lets you live your life without thinking about it, like your breathing and heart rate, as well as the metabolism of every single cell. With the signals out, the traffic goes wild. You can't fall asleep. Hello, walls.

Well, since you're up, let's dispense with a few more caffeine myths:

- Espresso has more caffeine than brewed coffee.

Sort of. One ounce of espresso can have three times the amount of caffeine when compared to one ounce of brewed coffee. But nobody drinks *one ounce* of brewed coffee. Instead, that eight-ounce cup can have 2½ times as much caffeine as that one-ounce espresso shot.

- Tea has more caffeine than coffee.

Sort of. On average, tea leaves can have almost double the amount of caffeine as coffee beans—but both brewed coffee and espresso have more caffeine because more ground coffee beans are used by weight to brew each cup.

- Caffeine is addictive.

No, although it is a stimulant. And once you get used to any happy jolt, you begin to rely on it. Like getting a raise. Or saying good-bye to your in-laws. But banking on something is not the same as being addicted to it. Going off coffee won't threaten your social, economic, or personal well-being. Instead, you may have headaches and increased irritability for a few days. Those are the symptoms of a dependency. They do not warrant the official, medical label of *addiction*.

- Caffeine can help you sober up.

Absolutely not. It's not as powerful as the alcohol in the vodka you just downed. In fact, coffee and alcohol are a dangerous combination. You *feel* more alert but you're still dead drunk. The only way to sober up is to stop drinking. But we'll get to the boozing myths later.

For now, you're still awake. Don't worry: there's darkness at the end of the tunnel. Caffeine hits its peak in the blood within two hours. After that, it falls off quickly, usually during the next hour. So go watch a movie. By the time it's over, you'll be sleepy—particularly if you've chosen some flick the hipsters have been raving about over their frothed-up coffee drinks.

SPICY FOODS COOL YOU DOWN.

JUST THE OPPOSITE, IN FACT.

This is the first of many myths based on an over-simplification or a misunderstanding of some basic facts. To understand its nuances, let's examine some scenarios.

It's 105°F, a hot summer day. You're roasting on the deck, quaffing a beer. You think, *Gosh, I could really go for nachos right now.*

Soon, friends arrive—with nachos! (Hey, it could happen.) You peel off a chip with a big jalapeño on top. You bite down and feel the burn. A trickle of sweat runs down your forehead. Sure enough, you shiver.

Listen, it wasn't the chile that made you chilly. In fact, that jalapeño warmed you up. It was the sweat that cooled you down. And that reaction may not happen every time. It depends on several factors.

Sweating leaves moisture on the skin. Moisture evaporates. Evaporation is a cooling process. The water "traps" the heat and then lifts off as a gas, pulling the heat away from you. The sweat dries; you feel cooler.

That is, in the best of all possible worlds. If you've been baking in the sun for a couple of hours and drinking nothing except one or two lousy beers, you're going to be pretty dehydrated—and you're not going to sweat that much.

What's more, any cooling process via sweat evaporation won't happen on a humid, muggy day. Or it will happen so slowly, your heat-stroked brain will get no relief.

Plus, a breeze has to stir the air to make the sweat evaporate quickly enough to do you any good. So if you're sweating outside on a 105°F day, and if you're properly hydrated, and if it's a relatively dry day, and if you happen to feel a light breeze, you may feel a little chill after eating that incendiary jalapeño. But not *because of* the jalapeño.

In truth, eating almost always increases your core temperature. Blood rushes to your stomach during digestion. You don't cool off after eating a hamburger. In fact, you may feel warmer—even wilted on a summer afternoon.

But eating a chile is a different ball of . . . heat. The burn is caused by a chemical compound called *capsaicin*. Impress your friends with its real name: *8-Methyl-N-vanillyl-trans-6-nonenamide*. Or not.

Capsaicin raises your metabolism. Thus, your blood vessels dilate and carry more blood—specifically, out from the body's core and into those little capillaries along your skin's surface. There, the blood heats up your skin. You may flush. And in turn, sweat.

So the truth of the matter is that capsaicin *warms* you up. Your body then takes care of that problem with its own natural defenses. You sweat.

Unless you eat too many nachos. In which case too much blood will rush to your stomach and you'll feel hotter because of the digestive fiesta going on down there. But don't worry: the bathroom's probably air-conditioned.

FOOD PREPARED AT HOME IS SAFER THAN FOOD PREPARED IN A RESTAURANT.

YOU'D THINK SO, BUT NO.

More people get sick from food at home than from meals in restaurants.

First off, a restaurant gets inspected. When it fails, the matter becomes public record. The joint may get shut down with an embarrassing notice pinned to its front door. Thus, a restaurant has a profit motive to keep people healthy.

Second, good food safety is all about proper hand washing. Statistically, that happens more frequently in a professional kitchen than at home. How many times do you wash your hands while preparing dinner on an average weeknight?

Finally, the safety of food is a matter of its temperature—which must be *below* 40°F or *above* 140°F, the so-called "safe zones." That's partly why chefs walk around with an instant-read thermometer in their pockets. Chances are, you don't even own one of these gadgets at home.

Not that you should take the temperature of the stew that's been sitting on your dinner table for thirty minutes. If you've kept the lid on, it may still be above 140°F. And even if not, bad bacteria haven't yet had time to set to work. It's probably not going to make you sick. But it *might* if you leave it out on the counter all night and have it for lunch the next day—even if you reheat it back into the safe zone above 140°F, killing all the bad bacteria. Because the residue from once-proliferating-and-now-dead bacteria can be as bad for your stomach as the live bacteria themselves. And some of that residue can only be destroyed at temperatures beyond the reach of a quick reheating.

There's yet another reason people get sick more often at home: they believe culinary myths. They believe that they can shove a piece of meat in a marinade and leave it at room temperature for hours because *vinegar kills everything.* Or they believe that you can tell when a piece of meat is done by how it feels.

The solution to this culinary threat to your health is twofold:

- Wash your hands often when preparing food.

- Practice good temperature control: below 40°F (that's your fridge's temperature) and above 140°F (not at a boil but still hot).

All that said, the real threat to your digestive tract lies neither at home nor in restaurants but somewhere in between. Quite literally. It's the take-out and prepared meals that you have to look out for.

Sure, they're hot at the restaurant. But then a delivery boy puts your dinner on his bike, drives around, finally gets to your place, rings the bell, waits for you to answer the door and pay, and then hands it over. You unpack the food, go back to the TV, and finally eat the lukewarm, uh-oh food—at your own risk.

Or you pick up a prepared meal at the grocery store, shop around some more, put your dinner in your hot car, drive home, fire up the DVR, and eat the questionable, lukewarm food.

No amount of hand-washing can rinse off the number of bacteria possible in those take-out cartons.

MYTH #7

NEVER REFREEZE MEAT.

FEEL FREE—MOST OF THE TIME.

It's Tuesday. Your mother-in-law is coming for dinner on Friday night. You take the chicken out of the freezer, set it on a plate to catch the juices, and put the whole thing in the refrigerator.

It sits there all week, thawing slowly. On Thursday, you play bridge with her. By Friday, she's still not talking to you. And you're not cooking for that son of hers. He can eat cold cuts at her house.

Still, you're stuck with a thawed chicken in your fridge. What will you do?

1. Throw it out and be the profligate daughter-in-law she always thought you were.

2. Roast it anyway, eat the whole thing yourself, and get fat as she always said you would.

3. Put it back in the freezer, call a friend, and go out for a liquid dinner to salve your feelings, and end up in your town's drunk tank as she predicted you would.

The answer is *any of the above*. They're all perfectly fine from a culinary standpoint. In terms of your mother-in-law, you're on your own.

If food has been thawed in a 40°F refrigerator and maintained there for a day or two at 40°F or below, it can definitely be refrozen.

But note that temperature: 40°F. That's the safe point.

And that goes for power outages, too. When the lights come back on, if what's in your freezer is still partially frozen and if the temperature in there has not gone above 40°F, let the compressor kick in and refreeze the stuff.

As usual, we've got a few *howevers*.

• You will definitely lose moisture during the first thaw—all those juices on the plate in the fridge—and then again during the second thaw. You won't have the juiciest chicken imaginable. But next week, you can take some comfort in the fact that his mother doesn't deserve your best cooking anyway.

• The meat may develop ice crystals which will turn into that dreaded, desiccated freezer burn. Cut away those bits, even if you'd like to serve them to her on a silver platter.

• If the meat has been left out at room temperature for more than two hours, do not refreeze it.

- If, when you bought the meat at the store, either a sign or a label stated it was *previously frozen,* you can't be sure how it was thawed—that is, if it was thawed at the safe 40°F temperature. Do not refreeze this meat.

By the way, this whole refreezing fandango goes for leftovers with meat, too.

Take a container of chili out of the freezer on Monday and put it in the fridge, wait a couple of days, be "out of the mood" for chili on Wednesday, and put the container right back in the freezer.

Now look who's a frugal, savvy, and competent daughter-in-law after all.

OYSTERS ARE AN APHRODISIAC.

MAIS NON!

This one may have started with the movie *Spartacus*. Specifically, with dialogue like this:

Crassus: *Do you eat oysters?*

Antoninus: *When I have them, master.*

Crassus: *Do you eat snails?*

Antoninus: *No, master.*

Crassus: *Do you consider the eating of oysters to be moral and the eating of snails to be immoral?*

Antoninus: *No, master.*

Crassus: *Of course not. It is all a matter of taste, isn't it?*

Antoninus: *Yes, master.*

Crassus: *And taste is not the same as appetite, and therefore not a question of morals.*

Antoninus: *It could be argued so, master.*

Crassus: *My robe, Antoninus. My taste includes both snails and oysters.*

To which Antoninus should have replied, "Is that a mollusk in your pocket or are you just glad to see me?"

Okay, maybe one movie doth not a myth make. It's also been said this whole nonsense started with an alleged *resemblance*: oysters are supposed to look like a certain part of the female anatomy.

Whoever came up with that one needed to get out more often.

In truth, oysters are made up of water, protein, carbs, fats, minerals, natural sugars, and salts. Not a one is a known aphrodisiac. But every one is necessary to good brain functioning—which is a much bigger aphrodisiac.

Plus, oysters are expensive, a treat. You usually have them when you're really putting on the dog. You make a reservation at a fine restaurant, one with plush drapes and cut crystal. You arrive with your date. You order a dozen oysters. You tuck in. You savor the good life. Soon, you're happy. And a little frisky.

There's the aphrodisiac: the narrative, the story, the whole thing that swirled up in your head. *I work a temp job and make no money, I'll be paying this dinner off until I'm a hundred and fifty, I don't care, I'm having a good time, I'll take another sip of wine, I've forgotten my troubles, I deserve this, I think we should go back to my place, I think respect's really important, and no, you can't stay over because I have an early meeting.*

By the way, the same thing goes for all the other alleged culinary aphrodisiacs: chocolate, nuts, ginseng, turtle eggs, the testicles of any animal, or powdered rhino horn. It's all in your mind. And soon enough in your pants.

THE ADJECTIVES USED TO DESCRIBE THE SIZE OF SHRIMP MEAN SOMETHING.

BULL HOOEY!

All adjectives associated with the size of shrimp are mere ad copy. *Colossal, gargantuan, crazy-ass big*—these words are put on the sign so you'll stop and pay attention to that nice man standing at the fish counter waiting to sell you something.

In truth, shrimp are sized by how many of their tails make up a pound.

Yep, their tails. We in North America eat only the rear ends of these squirmy buggers. We knock off the heads and bodies, which, together, are about as long as those tails. Did you know that some freshwater shrimp can grow to be a foot or so by the time you take their heads into account?

But forget about the Nessies of the Red Lobster set. Let's focus on what you'll find at the supermarket. For proper sizing, you need to know how many tails make up a pound.

Now it gets complicated. . . . Because it's about math.

☞   If about thirty-five shrimp (tails) make a pound, we're talking medium-size shrimp, good for stir-frying and such.

☞   If twenty make a pound, we're talking much bigger ones, perfect for shrimp cocktail.

☞   And if ten make a pound, we're talking a knife-and-fork affair.

☞   Beyond ten per pound, we get into categories the industry calls *U*. As in *U-5*s. That is, it takes fewer than (or *under*) five shrimp (tails) to make a pound, each one ringing in at a little less than a quarter pound.

☞   And U-2s? We're back to the Nessies, each tail weighing in at a little over half a pound.

While we're debunking crustacean myths, let's also talk about *baby shrimp*. They aren't babies. They're full-grown shrimp that live in the icy waters around Newfoundland, Alaska, and Greenland. Although they usually run more than a hundred to the pound, small is still not young. They can take four years to reach maturity. They arrive in the freezer section of your supermarket shelled and precooked.

Which is a good thing, because these guys, like all shrimp, are easily overcooked. All are done when the flesh has turned pink, opaque, and slightly firm. For shrimp at thirty per pound, that's about 4 minutes on a grill over high heat. For those at twenty per pound, maybe 6 minutes. Overcooked shrimp turn rubbery, even squishy—that's nobody's idea of a good dinner.

But long before you get to the grill or stove, the only thing you need to know is how many shrimp (tails) make up a pound. You bet size matters. Just don't take anybody's word for it.

LOBSTERS SCREAM WHEN YOU BOIL THEM.

WTF?

Let's set up a culinary syllogism, shall we?

1. To scream, something must have vocal cords.

2. Lobsters don't have vocal cords.

3. Lobsters can't scream.

End of discussion.

So what's the high-pitched whine you sometimes hear when you drop a lobster in a pot of boiling water? Superheated vapors whistling out from the joints in the shell.

In the end, this culinary myth is probably the result of anthropomorphization, a common fault with us humans and our cortex overflow. We have more brainpower than we need. You can probably think of counter-examples, particularly among your co-workers. Trust us: the rest of us do.

Our brains saw away at this thing called consciousness, even when we don't need them to. We have to put all that thought energy somewhere. Mostly, we project it onto the world. Happy trees. Peaceful clouds. Screaming lobsters.

Um, no. Trees are not happy. Clouds are not peaceful. We are. But we pay it all forward. And end up with our food screeching at us.

In truth, this question about lobsters and their shrieks is really about pain, right? Do lobsters feel pain when they're boiled alive?

Probably not in the way you and I would. Back off PETA. We—and all mammals—feel pain because of a chemical reaction along nerve channels connected to our brains. We're *not* talking about emotional pain, caused mostly by dating; we're talking physical pain, a matter of the central nervous system.

Which is the very thing a lobster lacks. Truth be told, it's a fairly simple organism. Not as simple as a clam—which is no more than a mouth, a stomach, and an ass. (Sound like anyone you've dated?) But not as complex as a cow, a pig, or a politician.

Simple or not, lobsters are vicious beasts. They spend their lives picking fights. Inevitably, somebody gets a claw snapped off—and doesn't show the usual signs of mammal pain. Doesn't grab the limb, doesn't back away, doesn't flinch.

That's not to say a lobster doesn't have a nervous system at all or doesn't feel something akin to pain. Just look at all that flailing as you hold the creature over the pot of boiling water. It's a defensive posture. And intriguingly, it happens *before* the thing's put into the pot. As if it knows something.

It may be some sort of rudimentary dread. It may be mere intuition. But in either case, it's pretty complex. Chances are, a lobster has never seen a pot of boiling water. Chances are, it's never been in a kitchen. Chances are, it's never experienced heat. Yet it knows what it knows without prior experience. So pain in the way we experience it? The vast majority of marine experts say "no." But some sort of elemental dread? Perhaps— although that comes near to a projection on our part, too.

In the end, a lobster is one of the few animals you'll bump off in your kitchen. These days, we've left the job of killing meat to others. Sure, some people hunt. Or fish. But most of us are not present at the death of our dinner.

So the whole lobsters-scream projection is a result of our own complex issues swirling around this very real dread called *death*—as well as its connection to eating. Even if you're a vegetarian, you still eat something that's died; or if you're a raw-food maven, you put it to death *as* you eat it. We eat things that have already experienced the very thing we most dread.

We can't solve that foundational riddle of existence here. We can only acknowledge it.

PERFECT LOBSTER WITH THREE DIPPING SAUCES

Knocks off 4 lobsters

You'll need the biggest pot you can find—probably a wide 10- or 12-quart monster. Plus a steamer rack to go inside the pot. When steamed, lobster is less water-logged and thus tastier than when boiled. Plus, the timing is much more forgiving.

Tap water
2 tablespoons salt
Four 1¼-pound live lobsters
One or more of the dipping sauces (recipes follow)

1. Fill a huge stock or soup pot with about 2 inches of water and add the salt. Set the steamer rack in the pot, cover, and bring the water to a boil over high heat.

2. Open the pot and put the lobsters on the steaming rack, one on top of another. They must be alive. And they will flail. Some claim to hypnotize lobsters by rubbing their underbellies. (Really? A creature without a brain can be hypnotized?) And some put the lobsters in the freezer for 15 minutes to delay the flailing. But is it more humane to freeze to death? Look, you've got two choices: suck it up so the lobster won't have died in vain, or become a vegetarian.

3. Cover the pot and steam for 7 minutes. Then use big tongs to rearrange the lobsters, switching around who's on top, who's at what angle, all for even cooking. Cover and continue steaming for 5 more minutes. If you've got bigger lobsters, they'll take longer. Ones that are 1½ pounds, about 8 minutes more; ones that are 2 pounds, about 13 minutes more.

By the way, a red shell is not the best indication that a lobster is done. After the right amount of time, crack one of the lobsters open where the shell meets the body and check the meat. It should be white, not translucent. If it's a female, there will be roe (egg sacks) running down the tail. The roe should be red and firm, not black.

Transfer the lobsters to serving plates and enjoy them with one or more of these dipping sauces.

Melted Herb Butter

Melt 2 sticks of unsalted butter with a sprig of fresh tarragon and a couple of smashed, peeled garlic cloves in a little saucepan over low heat. Remove the herbs and garlic, then use a spoon to skim off any foam. Spoon up or pour off the clear liquid in the pan, leaving the gunky white milk solids behind. Discard these in favor of the clarified fat.

Easy Cocktail Sauce

In a large blender, combine and blend: 1 cup tomato juice, 2 tablespoons jarred prepared white horseradish, 2 tablespoons Worcestershire sauce, 1 tablespoon tomato paste, 1 tablespoon lemon juice, and several dashes hot red pepper sauce, such as Tabasco sauce.

Chimichurri Vinaigrette

Purée all of the following in a large food processor fitted with the chopping blade: ½ cup olive oil, ⅓ cup packed parsley leaves, ¼ cup red wine vinegar, 3 tablespoons packed oregano leaves, 1 teaspoon dried red pepper flakes, 1 teaspoon salt, and 4 slivered garlic cloves.

2

YOU'RE SO CUTE WHEN YOU'RE DRUNK
Myths About Alcohol

Given that booze is one of our few legalized drugs, it's not surprising that it has come in for its share of tall tales. After all, alcohol has led to ill-advised marriage proposals, that third kid you really didn't want, and far deadlier consequences.

Sure, it alters reality. (*Has anyone ever told you that you look exactly like Brad Pitt?*) Sure, it makes bad ideas seem doable. (*Dude, we can install that skylight in your roof right now!*) And sure, it renders the idiotic rational. (*Do you have any Band-Aids? Because I just skinned my knees falling for you.*)

But there are some equally lamebrained myths about alcohol. So let's try to set the record straight. Or as straight as we can after testing the effects of alcohol . . . you know, in the name of food science.

MIXING LIQUORS WILL GET YOU DRUNKER.

DOESN'T WORK LIKE THAT.

Mixing liquors can make you sicker the morning after, but not drunker the night of the bender.

The intoxicating beverage you're currently knocking back is more than just a big swig of mind-altering chemicals. There are also various sugars, flavor esters combined with other tasty compounds, some chemical leftovers from the distilling process, some renegade impurities, maybe preservatives such as sulfites, maybe yeast dregs, maybe wood residue from the casks, maybe metal bonding compounds left over from joints in the still, and lots of water. The bulk of the stuff's water.

None of that will get you drunk. Yes, some people claim to have gotten drunk off water. But so-called *water intoxication* is not honest intoxication. It's a toxic reaction from ingesting too much water, gallons too much, a reaction that can lead to waterlogged cells exploding throughout your body. You're not drunk; you're dying. Sometimes, it's easy to get the two confused.

What gets you drunk is the one remaining component in the glass: ethanol, the sweet stuff that makes Uncle Fred wear a lampshade on his birthday and the fuel alternative that midwestern senators love to shill.

Truth is, ethanol is ethanol, no matter if it's found in three-hundred-dollar cognac, two-buck chuck, or that bottle of vanilla extract in your mother's pantry. The more ethanol you drink, the drunker you get.

However, that's not the end of the story. As we've said, you're knocking back more than just ethanol in that fussy cocktail, that glass of wine, or that bottle of beer. In fact, the other things in the mix—particularly the sugars and flavor esters—are the real reason you imbibe that tasteless ethanol at all. Unless you've had a particularly hard day.

Cheapo booze can have dozens of additional toxins: grain or sugarcane residues, free-floating chemical compounds, fertilizer leftovers, pesticide remnants, ground-water effluvia, and even soil contaminants. Some can survive repeated distillings.

You chug them all in that drink, along with the ethanol. You might react to some of them and not to others. Some might react with others already inside you. You then sit down to dinner and throw back some wine with its own sulfites, its different sugars, its own chemical signature—and you're most likely heading for a nasty hangover, depending on many factors, including personal sensitivities and allergies.

Sure, you're tipsy. That's from imbibing so much ethanol, not from mixing liquors. But your attempts at becoming the mad scientist of the bar, tossing concoction on top of concoction, may eventually get you into trouble when those other things in the drinks start a brawl in your gut—and in your head.

The best solution is better liquor. You get what you pay for. With higher-quality booze, more impurities are removed and fewer chemical shenanigans happen with the fruit or grains. If you plan on hopscotching from drink to drink all night, don't go with the well liquor. Pony up for the good stuff. But even spending down your IRA won't solve all your problems. So brace for tomorrow.

TROPICAL PITCHER PUNCH

Makes about 8 servings, depending on the size of your pour

So we've talked about the quality of the liquor you imbibe. But how do you know the quality outright? First off, don't simply rely on price. It's a good indicator, but not a perfect one. And don't go by labels. Remember: they were designed to attract you. A great bottle of artisanal tequila may have a rather work-a-day label. Scope things out: read distillers sites, check out reviews, and shop at a liquor store where someone can actually answer your questions. That person is your best guide to what's good on the shelf. If they seem surly or uninformed, take your business elsewhere.

1 cup white rum
1 cup pineapple juice
1 cup orange juice
½ cup brandy
½ cup amaretto or almond-flavored liqueur

¼ cup gin
1 tablespoon lime juice
Lots of ice

1. Mix all the liquids in a big pitcher. It's best to stir it quickly and thoroughly with a long-handled wooden spoon. But don't add ice at this point. And if you're not serving it right away, do not store the punch in the fridge. Instead, cover the pitcher with plastic wrap and set it aside at room temperature. But because of the natural fruit juices in the mix, don't plan on saving it more than 24 hours on the counter. Not that it would last anyway.

Two notes: 1) white rum is clear rum, sometimes called *silver rum*, as opposed to so-called *gold rum*, which is simply the same thing with food coloring added. Neither is the same as aged rum, truly stained dark by the wood casks— and a waste in a drink like this, better for sipping on its own.

2) Brandy is a fruit distillate, most often made by distilling wine. You don't want a fruit brandy from anything other than grapes for this libation, nor do you want a long-aged brandy. Look for a high-quality brandy, perhaps aged a little in casks, but not necessarily. Some brandies also have coloring added to make them appear to have been aged in wood.

2. When you're ready to serve the punch, add ice to the pitcher and stir like mad. You're using that pitcher as a large cocktail shaker. The perfect balance comes when ice melts into the punch—which is why you haven't stored it in the fridge. Fill tall glasses with fresh ice and pour the punch on top. Again, the melt is key. It will balance the many flavors and many kinds of alcohol.

MYTH #12

DARK-COLORED LIQUORS WILL MAKE YOU DRUNKER THAN LIGHT-COLORED OR CLEAR ONES.

NOT IN THIS WORLD.

Once, we were teaching a paella class on a cruise ship. As we sat down at a table and dug into our creations, a waiter offered red wine around the table—to the horror of one of the students.

"I can't drink a dark-colored liquor in the middle of the day!" she said. "I have to be functional for the bridge tournament. I'll just have vodka."

We didn't stop by later to see if she was the Queen of the Ace Trumpers. But as we've discussed, ethanol is ethanol, no matter its vehicle. Yes, there are some so-called *denatured alcohols,* found in mouthwashes, many of which are a whopping 27 percent alcohol.

Don't fool yourself. *Denatured* just means junk has been added to the ethanol to make it undrinkable, if not deadly— all so you don't down a bottle of mouthwash after a bad day at work.

Basically, ethanol is brain food. It percolates into your head, causing certain up-top neurons to fire repeatedly and quickly—but without much recourse to the brain's memory centers. Your cortex is in overdrive but your hippocampus is in neutral. You're in a graduate seminar *and* a coma ward. (Although no one's ever really sure of the difference.)

Every form of liquor has colorless, flavorless ethanol in it. Yes, ethanol does have a bunch of aliases: ethyl alcohol, grain alcohol, hydroxyethane, or ethyl hydrate. That's $C_{18}H_{27}NO_3$ for all you geeks who were paying attention in chemistry. But every single molecule adds up to intoxication.

Still, no alcoholic beverage is pure ethanol. If you'd like to determine how much is in a particular bottle of wine or beer, look on the label. The percentage is stated outright.

The labels of hard liquors such as vodka and rum offer instead their *proof.* In the eighteenth century, British soldiers were often paid in rum—which was usually diluted. To determine its purity, it was mixed with gunpowder. Too much water in the mix and the gunpowder wouldn't fire. Just the right amount and it still would—thus, the rum was *proofed.*

These days, the proof indicates a number double the percent of ethanol in the bottle. Vodka is 80 proof; therefore, it's a whopping 40 percent ethanol. If wine is, say, 12 percent alcohol, you'll be more tipsy after one four-ounce glass of vodka than after three four-ounce glasses of wine.

How tipsy? That'll depend how much ethanol you actually ingest based on serving sizes and your food intake for the past hour or so, how much water you've drunk between rounds, how high your tolerance for ethanol is, how long it takes you to imbibe what you've got in hand, how speedy your metabolism is, and maybe what your body-mass index is. But tipsy nonetheless.

ALCOHOL DESTROYS BRAIN CELLS.

NYET.

Although it's an article of faith among the schoolmarm set, this myth is a rank overstatement. If it were true, almost every novelist would have quit producing work in their early thirties. Faulkner? Nothing after *The Sound and the Fury*. Fitzgerald? Nothing after *The Great Gatsby*. Tennessee Williams? Nothing ever.

In fact, some evidence suggests that a small amount of alcohol momentarily *improves* cognitive function, probably by nixing the background hiss of inhibitions that effectively mute so much of our conscious thought.

That doesn't mean alcohol makes your smarter. After the first glass, you're as smart as you always were; you're just less likely to second-guess yourself. But don't go nuts. After the second or third glass, the ethanol begins to impair the tendril-like connections between your brain cells, those message-carrying dendrites. Thus, you slur. Thus, you stumble. Thus, you end up getting married in Vegas.

Too much alcohol in one sitting will not only make you *Mad Men* tipsy, it will also render the memory center in your brain pretty dormant. That's why you can come up with the idea for the world's greatest novel after the first glass of wine, be convinced you'll be the next John Grisham by the second, and not remember the plot the next morning.

Truth be told, brain cells are tough little buggers. They don't just roll over and die. However, if you knock them senseless enough times over many years—and we're talking about Russian levels of alcoholism here—you will end up with an atrophied brain. So the schoolmarms were wrong. Alcohol consumption doesn't necessarily kill brain cells; incessant, long-term alcoholism can.

There is still hope. Recent research suggests that even long-term *but moderate* alcoholism can be counteracted. Over time, those dendrite tendrils can be cleansed of the pasty gunk stuck in there from all those cocktail parties. Time itself appears to be the key. The gunk may decay; the tendrils may swim free. But it doesn't always happen—for still uncertain reasons.

Hard-core alcoholism is another matter. It can lead to a host of hideous problems, including Korsakoff's psychosis, a sort of blank brain, where the cortex has been completely divorced from the hippocampus. New information is not stored in the memory.

And yes, a minority of people do sober up after years of *moderate* alcoholism and complain of being addled. It's hard to tell whether that's a function of age (we're always more addled as the years pile up), genetic factors, or a real result from the days of wine and roses, with the gunk still refusing to decay.

In fact, the answer could vary from individual to individual.

In the end, don't worry about having a couple of drinks with your friends on Friday night. You'll still be the smarty-pants you always were. But you're on your own when it comes to remembering that brilliant idea for the world's greatest novel.

ALCOHOL WARMS YOU UP.

NICE TRY.

Having banked your pennies, you've finally made it to St. Moritz for the skiing vacation of a lifetime. You're staying at this snazzy little inn. After too much fondue one evening, you pull your car out of the parking lot to go for a winter drive. The moon is brilliant on the snow. Life is good.

Then you hit a patch of ice.

You skid off the road. Your car lands upside down in a ditch. You crawl out of the broken window. How will you survive?

Not to worry. That kindly Swiss innkeeper has seen it all, standing at your bedroom window after rummaging through your underwear. He's headed downstairs to send out the faithful Saint Bernard. Soon enough, you see the big dog loping over the drifts.

The furry fellow sits next to you with a little barrel strapped to his chest. You're saved! You smile, undo his collar, and release that blessed wooden token of Swiss hospitality—which you pocket for later. Then you hug the dog to warm up before hitching a ride back to the inn, where you plan on getting sloshed and passing out.

Yes, alcohol may make you feel momentarily warmer. More blood flows to your extremities, particularly as the tiny capillaries in your skin dilate. But that reaction is strictly temporary. The increased blood in your skin is ultimately dropping your temperature. The blood comes to the surface and makes you flush. But it's freezing outside. Your skin is cold. The blood quickly cools and returns to your core. Where it robs you of heat. That booze didn't warm you up; it ultimately chilled you down.

And because the alcohol has impaired your judgment, you're too drunk to notice the brrr. So now you're at a greater risk of hypothermia. Which is another reason alcohol is a poor way to warm up.

The whole Saint-Bernard-with-brandy-in-his-barrel gimmick was a crock. The Swiss knew the secret all along. It's that fireplace back at the inn that thaws the chill. When they come inside from the cold, they might down a brandy. They might even do it because they claim it warms them up. But they do it in front of a crackling fire. And *that's* what keeps them warm.

ALL THE ALCOHOL COOKS OUT OF A DISH.

NOT ON YOUR LIFE.

Although this doozy helps assure your Aunt Alice that your Uncle Fred won't get bombed on your wine-laced gravy at the next holiday dinner, the whole thing is oenological hogwash. Every dish made with booze still has ethanol in it. Sometimes, upward of every molecule dumped in. In a braise, stew, or sauté, the amount of ethanol left after cooking looks like this:

1 minute at a full simmer—85%

5 minutes—55%

15 minutes—40%

30 minutes—35%

1 hour—25%

2 hours—10%

3 hours—5%

5 hours—4%

7 hours—3.75%

If you've got guests who need Prohibition-friendly fare, substitute these for the hooch:

☞   Unsweetened apple juice or white grape juice if the point is to increase the sweetness of a dish;

☞   Chicken or vegetable broth if the point is to increase the savoriness.

So with all the personal, social, and religious conflicts possible, why use alcohol when you cook in the first place?

Ethanol can break down long-chain flavor compounds, the ones not easily dissolved in water. Most mammals still go for these long-chain proteins. Which is why your dog would prefer that you not cook that strip steak, even in a wine sauce.

But because of complex changes instigated by our use of fire to cook food, we humans taste short-chain compounds better than those long-chain ones. Heat snaps the chains apart. Alcohol, too. So it makes more flavor accessible to our flame-coached palates.

That said, a little wine isn't going to do much for, say, sautéed asparagus. That's because the vegetable's flavor molecules (sugars, starches, and such) are pretty simple, like the organism itself.

However, the same bit of booze will make a huge difference with chicken, beef, lamb, pork, veal, or venison, as well as salmon, halibut, shrimp, or lobster—all of which have long protein chains, soon to be zapped into more tasty bits.

But that's not all. Ethanol also has a tenderizing effect on meat. It relaxes the fibers, the same way it acts on your joints on an average Friday night.

All of which means you don't want it to boil off. You want it to stick around in the pan, working its magic, even while you're knocking back another glass.

RED WINE LOWERS YOUR CHOLESTEROL.

IT'S NOT THAT SIMPLE.

Red wine *can* lower your cholesterol. But it's not just red wine. It's also white wine, rum, and every other libation out there. It's what's in them.

Yep, we're back to ethanol. Just look at all its benefits. It makes you funnier. It makes you like your children again. And it increases certain protein transfers in the blood, thereby aiding the liver in raising the good sort of cholesterol.

In other words, ethanol improves your overall cholesterol ratio by raising your HDL, the high-density stuff that's so tough it polices the blood, picking up the bad crap—the LDL, the sticky, low-density stuff—and taking it back to your liver for processing.

The average bottle of wine has about sixty-five milligrams of ethanol. A man can down about half the thing, a woman about a third, and get the good benefits of ethanol—for medicinal purposes only, of course. You could do the same with a finger or two of vodka, although we would personally argue that the pleasures of a glass or two of wine at dinner are profound.

So are the problems. While wine is loaded with sugar, it's also acidic, with a ph from 2.9 to 3.9. That puts it pretty near some types of vinegar. You take a sugar, you add an acid, you give it to your liver, and bah-da-bing-bah-da-boom, you've got lots of triglycerides floating around in your blood—and potential issues with high blood pressure, obesity, liver disease, and maybe diabetes. Buyer, beware. Drinker, too.

But it's not just the ethanol, you may say. *I've heard about some miracle antioxidant in red wine, too.*

Yep, reservatrol. It may—*may*—have certain cardiac benefits and may—*may*—help prevent damage to blood vessels. In fact, it may—*may*—reduce (yes, reduce) your LDL count, the bad cholesterol.

But the research on the subject has only been conducted on mice. And the amount given to those besotted rodents would translate to your downing around a thousand bottles of red wine a day. That's one bottle every ninety seconds, all day, around the clock, nonstop. Not to sound like your grandmother, but don't you have something better to do?

Look, don't pretend you're quaffing red wine because a doctor told you to. Instead, have it with a meal to savor its complex flavors. Or just have a glass or two to enjoy life. But don't make pleasure medicinal. That's so 1957. Or 1597.

WHITE WINE HAS LESS ALCOHOL THAN RED.

SOMETIMES YES, SOMETIMES NO.

True enough, all is not equal in the world of wine. There are some bottles with 10 percent alcohol, others with 12, and still others with a whopping 14 percent. But it's an oversimplification to claim white wine has somehow less ethanol ounce per ounce than red. Here's the breakdown, in a general sort of way:

☞ Around 10 percent, you'll find German Rieslings, Vouvrays, and a host of rosés.

☞ Around 12.5 percent, you'll find Austrian Grünerveltliner, white Bordeaux, white Burgundy, New Zealand Sauvignon Blanc, Spanish Alberino, and French champagne, as well as Beaujolais, red Burgundy, Chianti, Rioja, and many lighter California reds.

Around 14 percent and even higher, you'll find California Chardonnays, Viogniers, Sauternes, as well as Pinot Noirs, California Cabs, Côtes du Rhône, Barolos, Syrahs, Malbecs, and Zins.

So you see that whites predominate at the low end of the spectrum, but they also exist at its top. Some white wines have less alcohol than most reds, but many reds have less alcohol than some whites.

And here's a further complication: most vintners in the late twentieth century started leaving grapes on the vines for longer and longer periods of time, harvesting them when the flavor compounds were more developed. The winemakers ended up with a fuller taste but also more alcohol, often the result of the increased sugars in the grapes. In other words, there are some powerful whites—and reds—out there these days.

And while we're on the subject of white wine vs. red, there's a similar myth about the number of calories in a glass of wine: that white has fewer.

A five-ounce glass of wine (a fairly standard amount) has between 100 and 165 calories. The difference is based largely on the amount of residual sugar in the wine, as well as the amount of ethanol, itself caloric (and derived from sugars).

Thus, the number of calories has little to do with the wine's color. Champagne, a light-colored wine, has more calories than almost all red wines because it has more sugar (and often more alcohol, too). Sweeter German wines like Auslese can have less ethanol but more calories. And sticky-sweet, white dessert wines can easily have more than 225 calories per glass.

Color is not an effective guide for anything except . . . well, color. If we'd known that earlier, we could have saved ourselves the trouble of quaffing white when we wanted red— as well as several centuries of human misery.

OPENING A BOTTLE OF WINE ALLOWS IT TO BREATHE.

SORTA.

You complete an enormous project, settle in for a wonderful dinner at Chez Snoot, and splurge on a 1990 Gevrey-Chambertin. The sommelier opens the bottle to let the wine breathe. You sigh. You're treating yourself right.

Too bad you did nothing for the wine.

No doubt about it, air is good for wine. Or more precisely, oxygen is good for wine. Back at the vintners in Burgundy, that wine aged because oxygen seeped in through the barrel staves as the grape juice morphed into the height of Western civilization.

But once the wine was bottled, it stopped picking up oxygen and started losing it, mostly through the cork. Meanwhile, the tannins slowly reacted with other compounds to form new flavors, themselves far less bitter.

So inhale, exhale: both are important. And you *should* let wine breathe before you drink it, particularly red wine, and particularly an older vintage. For several reasons:

☞ The wine absorbs a bit more oxygen, which continues to enhance its flavor profile, softening more tannins.

☞ Particularly in older, cellared wines, a little of the ethanol evaporates away, thus leaving you with a less "alcoholic"-tasting drink.

☞ Most modern wines include sulfites as preservatives; these can create stinky gasses over time and need to be released from the bottle.

☞ Aerating wine volatilizes many flavor compounds, which then reach your nose more quickly, floating around over the surface of what's in your glass. The good life just got better.

Unfortunately, none of this happens through the neck of a bottle. Or so little of it happens as to be meaningless. If you want to work on the flavor of a wine—and here we're once again mostly talking about a red wine with its pronounced tannins and sophisticated flavors—give it lots of surface area to interact with oxygen. In other words, pour it into a large, wide decanter so that the wine comes into contact with as much air as possible.

Also, pour it from a nice height, allowing it to splash about, exposing more air to its surface and allowing the evaporation of some excess ethanol.

Now the wine can breathe.

And yet you say you've experienced this happening in the bottle. *By the second glass, it was definitely better.*

No, *you* were better. When you first drink red wine, you might feel a slight prickle on your tongue from the ethanol. Also, you might pucker over some undeveloped tannins. But you quickly acclimate. You bypass those first sensations in favor of deeper complexities.

Plus, you've drunk from the bottle, exposing more of the wine's surface area to the air.

And you've had a glass of wine. You're loosening up.

No wonder the second glass was better.

3

NOTHING SIGNALS KNOW-HOW LIKE AN UPTURNED NOSE

Myths from the Fevered Brains of Culinary Snobs

Food snobbery invades our kitchens in so many ways; but it seems that the more common the item, the more pernicious the myth—and the more adamant the proselytizers.

Once, after a few cooking demos at a food festival, we wanted to kick back with a drink and good gab. We spotted some culinary brethren and sistern leaving our hotel. One group was going to a bar for beer and darts; the other, to a tony restaurant where the "foie gras beignets" were supposed to be "killer."

Hmmm . . . which group should we join?

As we were chatting, one of the foie-gras folks approached us on the QT. "I really enjoyed your demo," she said. "But

I was wondering about the chocolate. I noticed you weren't chopping it with the grain."

There it is: culinary frippery with no point except the sound of its own voice—and the making of myths that cause ordinary people to be afraid of their own pots and pans. Hang out with these snobs long enough and you'll think your dinner is sneering at you.

Listen, chocolate doesn't have a grain! And even if it did, we were melting it, so it wouldn't matter.

You can probably figure out which group we ended up joining.

MYTH #19

NEVER CUT LETTUCE WITH A KNIFE.

DON'T MAKE US LAUGH.

Lettuce is pretty sturdy stuff, botanically related to sunflowers and daisies; it doesn't need to be handled with kid gloves.

Back in the '70s and '80s, the snobs said you shouldn't cut lettuce with a knife because it would brown more quickly. The rationale went that if you tear lettuce by hand, you'll rend it along its natural seams and veins, thereby exposing fewer cells to the air and thus reducing the risk of oxidation.

Problem is, there's no evidence that hand-tearing lettuce rips apart fewer cells. In fact, there aren't fewer in the veins and rifts. Often, there are more, packed in to hold the plant together.

Test the myth at home. Tear some lettuce leaves; knife others. Save these salad fixings separately in your hydrator. Voilà, they'll both turn brown at about the same rate, probably in a little less than a week.

These days, the snobs have changed their tune. Maybe they did their own experiments. They're more apt to say that you shouldn't knife through lettuce because "hand-torn leaves look better on the plate."

But then you'll miss many of the table's finest salad offerings: an iceberg wedge with blue cheese dressing; a crunchy, chopped salad; or a good Caesar with those knifed squares of Romaine poised in the bowl.

Of course, the torn leaves at the supermarket last longer because they're sold in plastic bags pumped full of nitrogen, displacing the oxygen, the stuff that turns the broken cells brown.

If you lack a nitrogen pump at home, your greens will go squishy fairly quickly. There's no way to stop them from wilting, putrefying, and eventually liquefying. But there are ways to slow down the onslaught:

- With the exception of leaves in those sealed, nitrogen-filled bags, remove lettuces from their original packaging. And remove the leaves from the nitrogen bags after opening.

- Separate any heads into individual leaves and pat them dry with paper towels since excess water can also contribute to their squishifying. Water is the necessary ingredient for all decay. Things in a bog rot; things in a desert dry out. See King Tut's mummy for more evidence. Or your relatives in Arizona.

- Line large, sealable, perforated vegetable bags with dry paper towels, then put the lettuce inside. Make sure the bags are big enough to hold the head or leaves comfortably. You can also make your own lettuce bag by poking a zip-closed bag repeatedly with the tip of a paring knife.

- Check the bags every few days, replace any damp paper towels, and dump out any liquid in the bag.

All of this helps, but you still have to eat the lettuce within a few days. Face it: there's no such thing as a two-week salad.

MYTH #20

NEVER WASH MUSHROOMS.

YOU GOTTA BE KIDDING.

Mushrooms are made up of around 90 percent water. You know this whenever you slice them, drop them in a dry skillet over low heat, and leave them be. Pretty soon, they've released enough water to slick the bottom of the skillet. That is, if they're fresh—mushrooms lose water the longer they sit around.

Part of the problem is that they have no skin. Plants have it. Animals have it. Even birds and bees have it. But not mushrooms. So they leak moisture all the time.

After a few weeks on the shelf, they're ready to slurp up some water. This natural drive is probably the origin of the myth: if they're already sponges, why exacerbate the problem by washing them?

The answer: Because they grow in what can politely be called *fecal matter*. Of course you have to clean them. Even wash them. Here's how:

Start by slicing off a little bit of stem to remove some of the dirt (or, um, whatever) still clinging to it.

From this point, the paths diverge. Your route depends on what kind of mushrooms you've got in hand.

For those with pronounced, dark gills (like portobello caps), feathery fronds (like hen-of-the-woods mushrooms), or delicate caps (like shiitake mushrooms), wipe them clean with a *damp* paper towel or brush them clean with a *damp* mushroom brush, a gadget sold at high-end kitchen stores. Be gentle. A hard swipe can take off a hunk of the skinless flesh.

For sturdier mushrooms such as white buttons or creminis, *rinse* them under cold running water in a colander set in the sink, washing off the nasty stuff. Jacques Pépin actually submerges them in a tall glass of water, then drains them in a colander or his hand, releasing the loosened debris down the drain.

No matter if you've brushed, rinsed, or soaked the mushrooms, pat them dry, especially if they're going straight into a skillet with some hot oil. Otherwise, they'll pop and spatter. And if they're to be deep-fried, the batter won't stick to them if they're damp.

Even dried mushrooms must be cleaned. Since they also have to be rehydrated, you can accomplish both tasks at once. Set them in a large bowl, cover them with boiling water, and steep for about twenty minutes. The water will turn brown, becoming *mushroom liquor.*

Once the dried mushrooms are pliable, drain them, then rinse the gills and blot the mushrooms dry with paper towels before slicing and using. But catch and save that soaking liquid; once strained through cheesecloth or a paper coffee filter, it's an excellent substitute for canned broth.

And finally, when it comes to *wild* mushrooms, whether fresh or dried, always wash and dry them thoroughly. Wandering wild animals have probably used them as a rest stop. Nobody wants *that* in their soup.

STORE COFFEE BEANS IN THE FREEZER OR THE REFRIGERATOR.

WRONG.

Walk in a coffee shop and look around. Professional roasters do not chill their beans. They stock them on the shelf and sell them at room temperature.

Still, some people insist on storing their beans in a chilly place like the freezer. Which is about the worst thing they can do. It locks ambient moisture inside each bean.

As you know, the air around you holds water vapor (a.k.a. humidity)—very little in Arizona, quite a bit in Florida. That ambient moisture is the natural enemy of roasted coffee beans. Water in any form breaks down the flavor aromatics and essential oils—which is why you brew the ground beans in water in the first place. But once the water has worked its magic, the grounds are spent. There's not much flavor left—except for a few bad-tasting chemicals.

By freezing the beans, you've locked humidity (a.k.a. water vapor) inside each one. It's as if you've put a mob boss in a jail cell with a mob informant. It's not a good scene.

Okay, so the freezer's out—how about the fridge?

The fridge is a *very* humid place. Soon enough, you've got flavor death on a mass scale. Plus, a fridge is full of odors. And the coffee beans are porous. Do you want your morning joe to taste like tuna-noodle casserole?

So how *do* you store coffee beans?

☞ First off, always work with whole beans, not ground coffee. Grinding breaks down much of what makes coffee flavorful. Grind the beans yourself at home and use them fairly quickly once ground, preferably on the same day.

☞ Next, buy whole beans in foil packets with a plastic, one-way knob that adjusts the internal pressure. Freshly roasted coffee beans give off carbon dioxide. If there's no adjustment knob on the package, the beans have probably rested in the open air for several days (if not weeks) after roasting to make sure they don't blow up their sealed bags with CO_2—which means they've also been slowly degrading over time. That said, the fancy pressure valve on the package is only effective if you buy beans directly from a roaster and brew them up within a couple of weeks. If you buy beans from a store where the packages sit on the shelf for weeks if not months, that valve is window-dressing, a cost markup that does little for the quality of the beans.

Finally, store coffee beans in their sealed packaging or a sealed container in a cool, dark place. Light and heat—like cold and damp—are also their enemies.

For the best taste, coffee beans should be used relatively quickly, within a couple of weeks of their roasting date.

Notice a trend here? No two-week salad, no four-week cup of coffee. We hate to break it to you, but the modern age of convenience lied to you. Yes, you can get many things faster, but you can't keep a lot of them any longer.

MYTH #22

YOU WON'T CRY WHEN YOU CUT ONIONS IF...

IF *IFS* AND *BUTS* WERE CANDY AND NUTS . . .

If you keep your mouth closed. Or if you suck on a lemon. Or if you eat a piece of bread. Or if you light a candle. Or if—yes, this one's actually out there—you put your head in the freezer every five minutes.

None of which effectively deals with why you cry: propanathiel sulfoxide gas.

Curiously, it's not actually in the makeup of an onion. Instead, the vegetable has an amino acid compound that functions as its defense. When the onion is threatened in some way (knives count), the compound gets released, goes into catharsis with others in the plant, and comes out as a gas that wafts up toward your eyes—which in turn react defensively. They tear, their thin blue line against a world gone propanathiel sulfoxidy.

Those tears interact with the gas to produce a small—very small—amount of sulfuric acid. Which burns. Think about it: normal tears don't hurt. At least not physically. These sting.

That should tell you something. Namely, that there are two related but not identical reactions: the tears (which are a minor nuisance) and the burn (which is a major one).

So how do you stop it all from happening? Food snobs offer five misguided methods:

1. Freeze the onion for five minutes before chopping it. The chill does slow down the chemical reaction in the onion itself, but only marginally. Besides, a cold onion is harder to hold—which means you risk cutting your finger off.

2. Chop the onion underwater. Stopper your sink, fill it up, and try it. It's about as easy as drinking a glass of water upside down to get rid of the hiccups. And another good way to cut your finger off.

3. Have a very sharp knife. Which cuts more quickly. It's not that the onion produces less gas when chopped; there's just less time over the cutting board. But chances are, if you're using really sharp knives, you're working more quickly—which means it's easier to cut your finger off.

4. Wear goggles. It does work. But you look like an idiot. Worse yet, the goggles can fog up—and then you'll cut your finger off.

5. A fan. You can set a little hardware-store fan on the counter and have it blow across the onion, thereby pushing the gas away from your face. Just don't angle

the fan upward, or the gas will blow *into* your face, you'll tear up, and cut your finger off. And don't stick your finger in the fan or you'll cut . . . well, you get the picture.

In the end, there's really only one sure way to chop an onion without tears: get someone else to do it for you.

TO EAT BETTER, SHOP THE PERIMETER OF YOUR SUPERMARKET.

ARE YOU NEW AROUND HERE?

Telling people to shop the perimeter of their grocery store is about as smart as telling them to go to doctors only on the first floor of a hospital.

Granted, that vaunted supermarket real estate may have been better back in the day. The perimeter of Sam Drucker's market in Hooterville probably had a pickle barrel, a few produce bins, and a butcher counter. And maybe it's still true in some foodie Shangri-La, where tofu elves frolic among the organic veggies.

But these days, supermarkets have caught on. They're retailers, after all. And one of the primary retail rules is *first seen, first wanted.* That's why mainline department stores don't put either their couture lines or those boring gray boxer shorts in their front windows. Instead, they put the stuff you're most likely to want: that smart little cocktail dress, that jeans and cashmere V-neck. This is the merchandise they're trying to move, the stuff they've bought in spades.

Same with grocery stores. The vaunted perimeter of your supermarket is landscaped with skyscrapers of breakfast cereals, barbecue sauces, and diet sodas. Because that's the stuff people instantly recognize and want. It's also the high profit-margin stuff, the stuff that the food retailers want to sell. Most supermarkets sell this prime real estate to the highest bidder.

As you skirt your store's rim, you'll undoubtedly find real food—but more, too. You'll come across extruded meat in the deli case (what part of a turkey looks like a football?), various *cheese food* products, and donuts that give donuts a bad name—not to mention shortening-frosted cakes, fried chicken, and sugar-packed drinks that masquerade as fruit juices. So much for the perimeter as the land of tofu elves.

Besides, by just skimming the store's rim, you'll miss so much real food: whole oats and grains, maple syrup, brown rice, dried beans, olive oil, nut oils, and good vinegars. Mostly, you'll miss quality nutrition, good food, and great values.

In the end, there's no simple shortcut to the real food in your supermarket. Here's our advice:

1. Go in as an informed consumer. Take your reading glasses. Read the ingredient labels. Check out the nutrition articles in print and on blogs. Also, download a couple of apps that can help you negotiate the modern supermarket.

2. Don't shop hungry. You're more likely to fill up the cart with eat-them-right-now snack cakes and such.

Plus, you're more likely to be taken in by label claims.
Remember: sugar-free is often just an excuse for high
fat; low fat is often just an excuse for added sugar.

3. And give yourself the freedom to buy a frickin' candy bar
once in a while.

HEATING OLIVE OIL
DESTROYS ITS BENEFITS.

NOT QUITE.

Those very real benefits come in two forms: the nutritional ones (that is, the monounsaturated fats that have been shown in some studies to reduce bad cholesterol in the blood) and the tasty ones (that is, the many esters and compounds that make olive oil so darn yummy). At home, in ninety-nine cases out of a hundred, you needn't worry about losing either. But we'll need to take them on separately, starting with the nutrition claims.

Recently, there's even been a spate of reports that heating olive oil turns it into a saturated fat. Or worse, a trans fat.

Far from it! In fact, the monounsaturated fats in olive oil resist the oxidization necessary for just such a transformation.

Yes, if you *repeatedly* heat olive oil to a *very high* temperature—as is done in commercial frying operations—*some* beneficial polyphenols will be destroyed and a *small* amount of the fat will morph into a trans fat. But that doesn't apply to you at home—unless you're running a commercial deep-fryer every night for crowds. But then you've got more problems than mere olive oil will solve.

Now on to the claim about destroying olive oil's great taste—and this is the one that really gets the food snobs roaring.

In fact, heating a mid-priced olive oil may break down a few of its flavor compounds, but by no means all of them. And many of those luscious flavors will go directly into the food being cooked.

So be fearless. If you want to sauté some tuna in olive oil to make a fresh tuna salad, use a high-flavored olive oil so that its luscious aroma infuses the fish. If you want to fry wild rice croquettes in olive oil, make sure you get a good sizzle in the skillet with a nicely heated olive oil so that the crust has that slightly flowery taste, very Mediterranean and utterly irresistible. And if you want to fry battered chicken breasts in olive oil, by all means go ahead. With its high smoke point (between 365°F and 420°F), it's the perfect medium to keep the white meat moist and delicious.

Which leads us to a discussion of the smoke point for various oils. That's the point at which the oil begins to smoke, a warning sign that it's about to ignite. Remember this: the smoke point is not the flash point—which is several degrees higher.

All smoke points are guides, not rules. Oils smoke based on a manufacturer's proprietary blend and refining processes, as well as the oil's age and more complicated factors such as the ratio among saturated, monounsaturated, and polyunsaturated fat molecules in the oil. In truth, there's no way to give an exact smoke point for every oil. You can give averages and markers, but not hard-and-fast rules.

As an oil begins to smoke, the first to go up are its impurities—for example, microscopic bits of olives in olive oil. A jug of cut-rate oil will almost certainly have more impurities—and probably a lower smoke point.

But don't take any oil willy-nilly right up to its smoke point. You want to keep it under that mark—for safety *and* taste. So 365°F is a great mark for deep-frying with olive oil.

In the end, olive oil is pretty sturdy stuff. Yes, you can destroy some of the flavor palette of expensive oils. If you've blown forty bucks or more on a liter of the good stuff, don't deep-fry with it. Enjoy it by the thimbleful on salads or crunchy bread. Otherwise, keep a good bottle of fragrant—even extra virgin—olive oil in your pantry and heat it up at will.

PEANUT OIL IS A TASTELESS FAT.

NOT EVEN CLOSE.

This myth has been an industry standard for years. Vast sums have been forked over to PR shills to push it on the general public.

Yes, some modern peanut oil is deodorized. And it's highly refined to give it a very high smoke point, the better for deep-frying. The deodorizing and refining may well destroy many of the original flavor compounds. But not all of them. The oil still has a *very mild* peanut flavor—and when heated, a *slight* peanuty aroma.

Back in the day, even the mass-market brands smelled more like peanuts. We're talking the '80s here. But times have changed. These days, people apparently want less, not more. Less taste, less aroma.

Not us. We want big, bold flavors. They lead to increased satiety with every bite. (If you want to know the science behind that claim, check out our book *Real Food Has Curves*.)

For even more flavor, go for the unrefined bottlings, available at many high-end supermarkets and almost all Asian grocery stores. Some of these oils remain cloudy at room temperature. A few even have peanut shards floating in the mix. All have a very pronounced peanut taste, terrific at the bottom of a stir-fry.

However, they will go rancid more quickly, as any less-refined oil will. You can't keep them a year or so in the pantry. Instead, store them in the fridge. They'll go solid in the chill, but you can leave them on the counter for twenty minutes and they'll loosen up, at least at the top of the bottle.

Be careful when cooking with them. They have a *much* lower smoke point, as any less-refined oil. Yes, you can throw an unrefined peanut oil in a very hot wok, but you must have all the other ingredients prepped so you can work very quickly. That oil will come up to a smoke point—and frighteningly beyond—in no time flat.

Refined, unrefined—it's all a trade-off, no? You can deep-fry chicken in refined peanut oil but not in the unrefined stuff without flash-firing your kitchen into a remodeling project. With refined peanut oil, you'll have really crunchy chicken because of the oil's high smoke point but distinctly less peanut flavor.

You can still savor the taste of less refined peanut oils. They'll add depth to stir-fries and all sorts of savory fare—and even a few desserts that need a real peanut taste. But in either case, there will be a peanut taste, whether slight or pronounced, no matter what any industry spin doctor claims.

PEANUT SHEET CAKE WITH AN EASY CHOCOLATE BUTTER CREAM ICING

Call it 20 servings

Even if you can't find a less-refined peanut oil, any bottling will lend this classic sheet cake a slightly nutty, even smoky flavor. With the chocolate on top, it's like some sort of sophisticated version of a peanut butter cup. Goes well with a fresh pot of coffee, too.

10 large eggs, at room temperature

1½ cups white granulated sugar

2½ tablespoons vanilla extract

1 teaspoon salt

1½ cups cake flour, plus additional for
*   dusting the baking sheet*

¾ cup peanut oil, preferably a less-refined
*   bottling from an Asian market, plus a little*
*   extra for greasing the baking sheet*

9 ounces bittersweet or semisweet chocolate,
*   chopped into small chunks*

28 tablespoons (3½ sticks) unsalted
*   butter, cut into small chunks*

4 cups confectioners' sugar

6 tablespoons cocoa powder

1. Position the rack in the center of the oven and preheat the oven to 350°F. Lightly grease the bottom and sides of an 11 x 17-inch, lipped baking sheet with some peanut oil dabbed on a paper towel, coating even the corners and seams. Add some flour, then shake and tip the tray over the sink to coat the whole thing. Knock out any excess flour.

2. Beat the eggs and sugar in a big bowl with an electric mixer at medium speed until the mixture is thick and tripled in volume, about 10 minutes, scraping down the inside of the bowl occasionally. The mixture should fall in pale, thick ribbons from the still beaters—ribbons that do not immediately dissolve into the batter in the bowl. Beat in 1½ tablespoons vanilla and ½ teaspoon salt.

3. Scrape down and remove the turned-off beaters. Use a fine-mesh strainer to sift the cake flour into the butter mixture in ¼-cup increments, folding each one with a rubber spatula and making sure it dissolves before adding the next.

4. Fold in the peanut oil in 2-tablespoon increments (in other words, in 6 additions for that ¾ cup measure). Use wide arcs, lifting the batter from the bowl's bottom and turning it onto the top. Rotate the bowl often.

5. Pour and scrape the batter into the prepared baking sheet. Rap it a couple of times on the counter to displace any air bubbles. Bake until lightly browned and set, about 22 minutes. Transfer to a wire rack and cool completely, about 2 hours.

6. Stir the chocolate in the top half of a double boiler set over about 1 inch of slightly simmering water below—or in a heat-safe mixing bowl set over a medium saucepan with a similar amount of water simmering over low heat. Keep stirring until half the chocolate has melted, then remove the top half of the double boiler or the mixing bowl, and stir off the heat until all the chocolate has melted. Cool for 10 minutes.

7. Scrape the chocolate into a large bowl. Add the butter, the remaining 1 tablespoon vanilla, and the remaining ½ teaspoon salt. Beat with an electric mixer at medium speed until smooth and creamy.

8. Beat in the confectioners' sugar and cocoa powder at low speed to form a thick icing. Spread this over the sheet cake by dropping it in mounds and gently smoothing them together. It may help to wet a rubber or offset icing spatula to prevent sticking. If you want to make the cake ahead of time, cover it lightly with plastic wrap and store at room temperature for up to 2 days.

ALL-PURPOSE FLOUR IS BAD FOR MAKING BREAD.

NOPE.

If this were true, most home cooks would make terrible bread—because most home cooks use all-purpose flour for bread!

First, a quick definition. When it comes to flours, they can be made from "hard" or "soft" wheats. While the words *hard* and *soft* have something to do with durability, they mostly have to do with the protein content of the wheat. The less protein present, the softer things get. (Feel free to use this as dating advice, too.)

All-purpose flour is a balanced combination of hard and soft wheats, resulting in a moderate protein content that's lower (and thus softer) than hard bread flour, but higher (and thus harder) than soft cake flour.

What all this should mean in real life is that bread that has been made with all-purpose flour may be a tad softer than bread made with bread flour. (Likewise, cakes made with all-purpose flour may be a tad firmer than those made with cake flour.)

But alas, it's not that simple. Not all all-purpose flours are created equal. There are various protein contents depending on the proprietary blends developed by different manufacturers. So here's the real deal:

☞   If the bread recipe calls for bread flour and all you have is all-purpose, you're still good to go—with a couple of changes that we'll get to in a second.

☞   If the recipe calls for all-purpose flour and all you have is bread flour, you need to go to the store. (But good for you for having a specialty flour in your pantry. You're probably the type who won't mind a trip to the store.)

For pitch-perfect aesthetics in your bread-making, here are a few tips to creating a crunchier loaf even with all-purpose flour.

1. **Add 1 tablespoon additional all-purpose flour for every cup of bread flour called for in the recipe. The extra protein in that little bit of extra flour will help give the bread a better structure.**

2. **Provide a warm, moist environment as the bread bakes so that the loaf rises quickly and then dries out. Spritz the oven with water right before the loaf goes in. That little bit of steam will work wonders. But avoid spritzing water into a gas oven—dousing the flame can be a recipe for disaster.**

3. **Bake the all-purpose loaf a little longer, maybe just a minute or two, to give it more surface crunch. Because a crunchy crust is the whole point, right?**

In the end, if you want to make bread from scratch, don't let the snobs scare you off. Sure, there's more to learn at every turn. But be prepared to get dirty and go for it! (Consider this more free dating advice.)

MYTH #27

YEAST MUST BE PROOFED BEFORE BAKING.

ALSO CONSIDER JOINING THE CALVIN COOLIDGE FAN CLUB.

The years between the flapper '20s and the psychedelic '70s were not kind to the food world. We suffered many indignities. Stirring food coloring into oleo margarine. Thinking mandarin oranges only came in cans. Considering hot Dr Pepper with a slice of lemon a sophisticated beverage.

This bit about proofing yeast is another blip on that timeline. To disprove it, we must tell the story of culinary yeast.

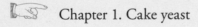 Chapter 1. Cake yeast

For about four millennia, give or take a year, this was the baking standard: a small block (or "cake") of yeast, the real deal, right out of a fermentation vat. Also called *compressed yeast,* this stuff is alive and highly perishable. These days, it's sold under refrigeration to try to preserve its integrity. It goes stale—that is, dies—quickly, sometimes in a matter of days. After being the standard for so long, it proved a tough sell to the F. Scott Fitzgerald set. These people were too busy making bathtub gin. So along came . . .

☞ Chapter 2. Active dry yeast

Hello, the Great Depression. Hello, Mother of Invention. And hello, yeast that doesn't need refrigeration, made by grinding yeast itself into little grains that are coated in a dust the industry calls *yeasty debris* (a.k.a. yeast poop).

This yeast is content but asleep, like a pig in . . . yeasty debris. Anyway, active dry varieties can be stored for months at room temperature, seemingly impervious to age.

To wake up, the yeast have to settle in for a nice, warm bath—that is, be sprinkled in a bowl of liquid that's between 100°F and 110°F, probably with a little sugar in the mix to get things moving. The yeast jump out of bed, stretch, chow down, and start producing gas. About like you after a cup of coffee and a bran muffin. Except they're producing carbon dioxide, the stuff that makes bread rise.

Despite the benefits of its increased shelf life, a yeast that needed proofing proved a hard sell to the Woodstock set. These people were too busy making bathtub LSD. So along came . . .

☞ Chapter 3. Instant yeast, including those branded as *rapid-rise, quick-dry*, or *bread-machine yeast*

Instant yeast is ground in even smaller granules than active dry yeast. It can be added directly to the dry ingredients *without* the additional step of proofing—because it's alive and thus needs to be refrigerated after opening (and maybe even before). Check the expiration date on your package to make sure it's still fresh.

Instant yeast produces so much carbon dioxide, way more than active dry yeast, that even a little bit will give off voluminous clouds. However, the liquids poured into the dough or batter should be between 100°F and 110°F to get the yeast moving. But proof it? No way.

So if you're still working with active dry yeast—and pressing your clothes with flatirons heated on your stove—then by all means, proof the stuff. But for the rest of us, the professionals working with cake yeast or the average home cook with instant yeast, we can forever be done with this myth born of a distinct, historical blip. And we can pour out the hot Dr Pepper, too.

MYTH #28

BUTTER MAKES FLAKIER BAKED GOODS.

NOT SO, BUT IT'S NOT THE END OF THE STORY.

Shortening makes flakier cookies and crusts. We're not talking about breads and cakes, but about things that need to be crisp in some way. Their doughs and batters are always a mix of some sort of flour and some sort of fat—which means they're a balance of glutens (the sticky protein structure in flour) and acids (which is what fats actually are).

The glutens are tough little superheroes. They love to flex their muscles. Left to their own devices, they turn sticky with the addition of water—and then dry out into little bricks.

Their nemeses are acids—in this case, fats. Which aren't just tasty. In batters and doughs, they're kryptonite to those little glutens. An acid keeps them in check.

That's why some bakers also add a little lemon juice or vinegar to the dough for a piecrust. Once again, more acid, less gluten strength—and thus, more flake per bite. Within reason, of course. You have to have some structure. Otherwise, you end up with pie in your lap.

Cookies are usually cakier than piecrusts because of the addition of eggs. But both have a similar structure: lots of layers of wheat glutens separated by thin sheets of fat. These sheets hold the glutens apart, allowing them to dry out in the oven's heat without bulking up and bonding together. Voilà: a crunchy cookie or a great crust.

Okay, so on to the match of the day: shortening vs. butter. Who will win?

☞ Round 1. Shortening is 100 percent fat. By contrast, butter is 80 percent fat with water and milk solids filling out the rest. The one with more fat (that is, acid) will be the one that permits less gluteny stiffness. And thus also makes flakier cookies and piecrusts.

Shortening wins the round.

☞ Round 2. Butter's big problem is its lower melting point. It liquefies more quickly and can run out before everything's dried out and crunched up in the oven. The best butter batters are rested in the fridge for a while to chill them down before the oven's inferno, mostly to give the butter a leg up. But there's no need for this extra precaution with shortening. It holds up to the heat, keeping its shape longer, and allows those flaky layers to form.

Once again, shortening wins the round.

☞ Round 3. Butter tastes better. Ever licked shortening off a spoon? Enough said.

Ah ha! Butter wins the final round.

In the end, you should probably compromise: use butter and shortening together, probably about a third butter and the rest shortening. Taste plus flakiness: a match made in heaven.

One more thing: butter-flavored shortening doesn't cut the mustard for us. Unfortunately, that artificial butter flavoring can be diacetyl, a known carcinogen with a slightly metallic taste. We'd rather just use butter. We'll take slightly less flaky cookies over those that taste like aluminum foil and might give us cancer. But maybe we're just weird that way.

CARDAMOM SUGAR COOKIES

Plan on about 4½ dozen cookies

Cardamom is the new cinnamon! At least, it ought to be. It's a warm spice, like nutmeg or mace, very deep-tasting, a long-lasting finish in these otherwise crisp, flaky wonders. As to how many cookies this recipe actually makes, just remember that large egg sizes vary by several grams, no one measures dry ingredients exactly the same way, and you might beat more or less air in the batter than we did. But close enough counts.

2¾ *cups all-purpose flour*
1½ *teaspoons cream of tartar*
1½ *teaspoons baking soda*
1 *teaspoon ground cardamom*

$1/2$ teaspoon salt

$2/3$ cup solid vegetable shortening, preferably trans-fat-free shortening, sold in the refrigerator case of most supermarkets

$1/3$ cup (5 tablespoons, plus 1 teaspoon) cool unsalted butter, cut into little chunks

$1^1/3$ cups white granulated sugar

$1/2$ cup packed light brown sugar

2 large eggs, at room temperature

2 tablespoons whole or low-fat milk

1 tablespoon vanilla extract

1. Position the rack in the center of the oven and fire it up to 375°F. Line a large baking sheet with parchment paper or a reusable silicone baking mat.

2. In a medium bowl, stir the flour, cream of tartar, baking soda, ground cardamom, and salt using a whisk or fork.

3. In a big bowl, use an electric mixer at medium speed to beat the shortening, butter, and 1 cup white sugar, and the brown sugar until smooth and creamy, 4 to 5 minutes, scraping down the inside of the bowl fairly often.

4. Beat in the eggs one at a time, making sure the first is fully incorporated before adding the second. Beat in the milk, then the vanilla.

5. Turn off, scrape down, and remove the beaters. Add the flour mixture to the bowl. Stir it in with a wooden spoon or a rubber spatula just until there are no pockets of undissolved white flour in the dough. Set it in the refrigerator for 10 minutes.

6. Spread the remaining ⅓ cup white sugar on a plate. Wash and dry your hands. Scoop up 1 tablespoon of the dough. Roll it into a ball between your palms, then roll it in the sugar. Set the ball on the prepared baking sheet; flatten it to a little less than ½ inch thick. Continue making more balls, rolling them in sugar, and flattening them on the sheet, spacing them a couple of inches apart.

7. Bake until crisp and brown, about 14 minutes. Cool on the baking sheet for a minute or so, then transfer the cookies to a wire rack to cool completely. Also, cool the baking sheet itself several minutes before making more cookies—if it's hot, they'll spread too quickly. Or work with two lined baking sheets. If you've used parchment paper, change it out for a fresh sheet if it's brittle. Once they're all made and cooled, you can store the cookies in a sealed bag or container at room temperature for up to 3 days, or in the freezer for several months.

MOLDY CHEESE SHOULD BE THROWN OUT.

WELL, MAYBE . . .

Here's another myth that's really a rank overstatement. The answer's *sometimes yes, sometimes no.* So how can you tell what kind of mold is safe and what's not? To answer that question, we need to take a quick tour of cheese.

☞ **To begin, the hard cheeses, such as an aged, crumbly Cheddar or Parmigiano-Reggiano.**

You don't want to eat *any* lurid molds on the surface of hard cheeses or any of those rare ones tunneling into the block. Those bits of fuzz and icky streaks are not part of the original culture. Cut them off, as far down as they go. The good news is that bad molds cannot easily penetrate hard cheeses. Thus, they usually remain in discreet veins, mostly on the exposed surface. If you cut them off with one-inch margins, you're safe.

☞ **Next, the semihard cheeses— Gruyère and Gorgonzola, for example.**

Same advice as for hard cheeses: cut off any foreign molds with one-inch margins all around. However, there's one complication: you have to know what's part of the original culture and what's not. Any blue veins in a blue cheese are original molds—and to be savored. Other bits of mold—like deep green stains or blotchy brown fuzz—have to go.

☞ *Then the semisoft cheeses, like Brie.*

These cheeses, particularly artisanal versions, do not get better with age. Instead, cheese makers release them at the moment of their perfection. A semisoft cheese should not have molds of any kind, *except* for the pale white, green, brown, gray, or dusty blue molds that the cheese maker has used to create the rind. Which, by the way, can replicate itself. When you slice into a semisoft cheese, it may redevelop those same surface molds on the exterior of the cut bits. Fine. You're still good to go.

However, if the cheese develops other molds, spotty green or blue ones in hairy hunks, toss the whole thing out, no cutting them off and no trying to save the cheese. These molds can penetrate like forked lightning into the soft interior. Better safe than sorry.

That's not the only time you should say au revoir to a semisoft cheese. If the top is collapsing at its center, the cheese is most likely beyond its prime. If the cheese has an ammonia odor, it's ready for the trash. And if it's bitter—not sour, but bitter—you're better off spitting it out.

As we said, some artisanal semisoft cheeses have blue, green, brown, or even gray molds on their rinds. These must be evenly distributed. If you're buying cheese from a reputable cheesemonger, you'll have the confidence to enjoy these bits of extravagance—but indulge right away, within a couple of days.

Finally, the soft cheeses, such as fresh chèvre, cream cheese, and cottage cheese.

These should not have any molds of any sort. The moisture content is so high that the molds can send imperceptible threads and veins down into the cheese. In all cases, throw out any that have grown any bits of discoloration.

In the end, remember that most cheeses, especially artisanal ones, are not long-term projects at home. They should be bought and consumed fairly quickly. So buy less more often and you won't have to worry much about those pesky molds that can ruin a good cheese platter, not to mention much more.

DIVER SCALLOPS ARE CAUGHT BY HAND.

AND MONKEYS MIGHT FLY OUT OF . . .

Diver scallops—the name itself really captures the imagination. You can just see some guy rolling out of his hammock, running his little boat out to the warm Atlantic waters, donning a mask, and plunging into the blue infinity. He brings up scallops one by one, tossing them into his rocking skiff. Later, he sells them at the dock and they end up on the menu at your favorite restaurant.

A romantic image for sure . . . until you snap out of your reverie and realize how many restaurants, grocery stores, and specialty food markets this guy must be stocking. Heavens to Murgatroyd, there must be a flotilla of these guys, bounding out of a zillion hammocks every day.

You've been had by window dressing. Just like you were with *jumbo shrimp*. Or *swimmer's build* from that online dating site.

These days, most scallops are grown on lines, as it is for commercially farmed mussels and clams. That's actually good news. They grow above the increasingly toxic sludge on the ocean floor. But every single one of those scallops dangling on those lines can be called a *diver scallop*.

It's an industry term that means they were not doped with sodium tripolyphosphate, a chemical that allows them to stay fresh longer. It also allows scallops to take on up to 20 percent additional water by weight. With this chemical tomfoolery, you end up with less scallop, more water, and a longer shelf life, all while paying about the same as for any other scallop.

So the words *diver scallops* could be a good thing: nothing's doped up. But they don't really say anything about sustainability, the way you might think. And sometimes, the words are just slapped willy-nilly onto scallops, especially since there's little to no governmental enforcement.

But don't despair. There are ways to avoid all this chicanery:

Look for dry-pack scallops.
These, too, have not been doped with the water-retention chemical. But the name is a bit more of a surety since it hasn't disappeared into glossy ad copy.

Ask questions of waiters and fishmongers
Questions that get real answers, not just nods, shrugs, and smiles. Where did these scallops come from? How were they harvested? When did you get them? If they were previously frozen, when were they thawed? And can I see the package they came in?

Know your supplier.

A quick Internet search will give you more information than you can imagine.

And one more note: the words *day boat* are also window dressing. A boat can go out, drag the ocean floor for scallops, and come in at night. Voilà: a day boat. It doesn't mean that the scallops were necessarily harvested in a sustainable way. Maybe so, maybe not. Once again, know the facts, talk to suppliers, and do some reading. Well informed is well armed—and more contented, to boot.

YOU CAN TELL IF A STEAK IS DONE BY HOW IT FEELS.

LET US KNOW HOW THAT WORKS OUT FOR YOU.

Ever heard this one? *It's medium-rare if it feels like the flesh between your thumb and forefinger.* Or: *It's medium if it feels like the skin on the bottom of your thumb at the palm.*

There are just too many factors involved to make sense of this tripe. How tight is the skin on your hands? How many marathons a year do you run? How many did the cow run? And how thick was that steak in the first place?

Then there's this problem, the biggest of all: one person's rare is another's well-done. Yes, chefs love to poke and prod. But whose notion of *rare* are we talking about? Theirs? Yours? Ever sent a steak back in a restaurant? We'll bet the chef thought it was cooked to your liking.

We were once teaching on a cruise ship and watched a steak come back to the kitchen because the diner claimed it wasn't really well-done. It was gray throughout. It looked like leather to us. But the chef put it back on the flat-top grill. It went out and came back again as unsatisfactory. He split it open and splayed it out on the super-hot flat-top grill. It went out and came back again. Then he dropped it in the deep-fryer for five minutes. What came back this time were the diner's compliments.

In the end, the only guide to meat's being done is an instant-read meat thermometer. And you need to know what the temperature it registers means. In the best of all possible worlds and with some misgivings, here are our guidelines for beef:

- Bloody (or *bleu* to the French): 116°F. Cool in the center, the proteins have not coagulated. A good vet might still be able to save the cow.

- Rare: 125°F. Warm throughout, red in the middle, the proteins just coagulated. Your foodie creds are safely intact.

- Medium-rare: 130°F. Warm throughout, a little graying around the edges, a lighter red, somewhat pink, in the center. This was '70s standard—and is still the grail for many grillers.

- Medium: 140°F. A larger gray band at the edges enclosing a still juicy center. Call it the midlife crisis steak.

- Medium-well: 145°F. Very little color left, often none, with some juice left. The edges will have desiccated and are in serious need of ketchup.

- Well-done: 150°F and up. Shoe leather but the gold standard among some cruise ship passengers.

And now for those misgivings—or our rank hypocrisy. Earlier, when discussing food safety, we claimed 140°F was the good-to-go temperature mark. It is. To that end, the USDA insists medium-rare is 145°F, twenty degrees higher than the guidelines we just gave you.

Yep, there are trade-offs. We eat beef outside those safe-temperature parameters because we like a hot, red, or pink center to our steaks. But we buy beef from producers whose hands we shake on a weekly basis, we buy from local farms near us, and we cook the meat very carefully.

But we're still running a risk. If you're eating feed-lot beef or dining in chain restaurants or even in small restaurants where there's just a cook, not a chef, go with the 145°F guide as your medium-rare. If however you've got your hands on better-quality steaks from high-end butcher counters or farmers' markets or you're eating out at a high-quality restaurant, follow our best-of-all-possible-world guidelines.

But in any event, do what you do by temperature, not by feel. And always know when you've passed beyond the limits of assured safety.

PERFECT STRIP STEAKS WITH BLACKBERRIES AND CREAM

Dinner for 2; double for a foursome

We call this method the *sear-and-shove*. Sear it on the stove, then shove it in a hot oven. It's the way most professionals cook—and you should, too. However, it does require good, sturdy cookware. To that end, we recommend a seasoned cast-iron pan—or failing that, a really heavy-duty skillet.

1 tablespoon olive oil
Two 8-ounce boneless beef strip steaks
½ teaspoon salt
1 tablespoon unsalted butter
1 medium shallot, minced
2 teaspoons minced sage leaves
¼ teaspoon ground cinnamon
¼ cup dry white wine or dry vermouth
¼ cup fresh blackberries (do not use frozen)
2 tablespoons heavy or whipping cream
½ teaspoon freshly ground black pepper

1. Position the rack in the center of the oven and preheat the oven to 400°F.

2. Rub the olive oil over both sides of the steaks and then season them with the salt, both sides. Those steaks may have little, fatty tails that curl around one side—or may have excess fat on one side. Leave it or trim it off, your choice.

3. Now the fun begins. Heat a large oven-safe skillet, preferably a seasoned cast-iron one, over high heat until it's smoking. Seriously. Smoking. Turn on the vent. Open a window. Put the kids and dog out back. A drop of water in the skillet should skitter and darn near explode on contact.

4. Slip the steaks into the skillet. And do nothing. Leave them alone for 4 minutes, until they get good and crusty on one side.

5. Flip the steaks and shove the skillet in the oven. Don't forget your oven mitts—everything's really hot. Close the door and leave the steaks in there until an instant-read meat thermometer inserted into the thickest center of a steak (without going through and touching the skillet) registers 125°F for rare, about 4 minutes; 130°F for medium-rare, about 5 minutes; or 140°F for medium, about 7 minutes. But remember that timing is no guide. And don't worry about poking the steaks with the thermometer probe and somehow letting juices run out. We'll get to that myth in a bit.

6. Use your oven mitts to remove the skillet from the oven. Transfer the steaks to two dinner plates. If you'd like, tent them with foil to keep warm. Set the skillet over medium heat and add the butter. Let it melt, then toss in the minced shallot. Stir the shallot around for a minute, just until soft, then stir in the sage and cinnamon for a few seconds.

7. Pour in the wine. It will almost instantly come to a boil. Stir quickly to get all the browned bits off the bottom of the skillet.

8. When the wine has reduced by half, stir in the blackberries, cream, and pepper. (Why so little cream? You don't need much.) Stir constantly just to warm the blackberries through, about 30 seconds; then divide the sauce between the steaks on the plates. Dig in!

YOU CAN'T LIFT THE LID WHEN COOKING RICE.

MAYBE ONCE UPON A TIME BUT NOT SO MUCH ANYMORE.

Although rice has been grown in the American Southeast for centuries, it was not a dinner-table staple across the United States until the early twentieth century, its widespread growth a product of both better transit routes and increased Asian immigration.

Its coming was not without difficulties. It quickly topped the list of the foods that terrorized our mothers and grandmothers, driving the average, post–Korean War house-wife batty as she tried to make the perfect rice her husband had once tasted in Asia.

To alleviate her anxieties, manufacturers developed a gaggle of convenience products: converted rice, instant rice, and boil-in-a-bag rice, to name three.

Still, there were those stalwart home cooks who yearned for the real thing. And yet were nervous. And felt that rice was temperamental, just like their husbands when they came home from Korea. And thus, we ended up with this whopper.

Listen, if you don't lift the lid, how do you know when the rice is done? How do you know if you've enough water in the pot to get the grains tender without their scorching? How do you know it's at the right level of simmer, bubbling away quietly? How do you know much of anything?

In fact, the rest of the world is not tied to its lids. Many East Indian cooks make rice swamped with way too much water, so much so that a lid doesn't matter; they then pour off the excess when the grains are tender. Spanish cooks make paella in an open pan. And Italians stir risotto with no lid in sight.

But when it comes to rice, North Americans follow what's considered *the Asian model*—that is, they cook the grains in just enough water that it boils away at the same moment the grains are tender.

There's a problem: *just enough water.* How much is that? The grains have varying amounts of residual moisture based on the rice varietal, the drying method used in production, the time the package has sat on the store shelf, and the ambient humidity in your pantry.

One answer is to use a rice cooker with a computer chip that adjudicates humidity and timing with the type of rice used. (Ours has never failed us.) But without that fancy gadget, when you're using a good, ol' saucepan on the stove, you have to lift the lid and check—because if you're following the Asian method as most North Americans do, you're trying to balance rice and water perfectly.

Is the water gone before the rice is tender? Add a little more and cook the grains a little longer. Is the rice tender but there's too much water in the pot? Then either drain off the excess by pouring the contents of the pot into a fine-mesh sieve for drier grains or leave the lid off entirely and cook off that excess moisture for stickier rice. Has the rice gotten done more quickly and the cooking water been absorbed or evaporated before the stated time on the recipe? Then you're ready to eat it now.

And now you should. Cooked rice is prone to a type of food poisoning associated with a bacteria found dormant on the grains. Sushi rice and some rice salads are safe because the added vinegar keeps the bad bugs from coming to life too soon and interfering with your fun. But err on the safe side: quickly refrigerate leftover, cooked rice.

CRAB PILAF

Dinner for 6

It sounds retro, but a pilaf is a wonderful rice casserole, perfect for an autumn evening—and an alternate third way to cook rice. Covered but in the oven, more of a sturdy, church-supper way. The sweet rice offers a lovely balance to the crab—which is so easy to use in recipes, thanks to the advent of pasteurized crabmeat in our supermarkets. No need for jumbo lump crab here, since you'll stir the dish and flake the meat anyway. But do first pick it over for shell shards and cartilage. Even the best processing can leave some behind. Spread the crab out on a plate and go through it gently with your fingers. But be careful: those bits can pierce your fingers. No matter what you do, don't buy dyed, artificial crabmeat. It won't have enough flavor to make a satisfying meal in this relatively simple casserole. A salad dressed with a vinaigrette goes alongside this dish nicely.

2 medium leeks
2 tablespoons unsalted butter
1½ cups long-grain basmati rice
2 tablespoons minced tarragon leaves
1 tablespoon Dijon mustard
½ teaspoon salt
½ teaspoon freshly ground black pepper
3 cups canned fat-free, reduced-sodium
   chicken broth, perhaps a little more
   depending how much the rice needs
8 ounces lump crabmeat, picked over
   for shell and cartilage

1. Position the rack in the center of the oven and preheat the oven to 350°F.

2. Slice off and discard the root threads from the leeks as well as the dark green leaves, saving just the white and pale green parts. Slice these in half lengthwise. Open them up under running water and rinse inside their chambers to make sure you clean out any dirt or grit. Set them cut side down on your cutting board and slice them into thin half-moons.

3. Heat a 2-quart, high-sided, oven-safe sauteuse pan or a large high-sided, oven-safe skillet over medium heat. Add the butter, let it melt, and then dump in the sliced leeks. Stir over the heat until they soften and turn translucent, about 4 minutes.

4. Stir in the rice. Keep stirring over the heat until the grains begin to look translucent at their edges, about 1 minute.

5. Stir in the tarragon, mustard, salt, and pepper. Cook for 30 seconds, then pour in the broth. As it comes to a simmer, scrape up any browned bits on the bottom of the pan or skillet. Bring the broth up to a full simmer, stirring occasionally.

6. Gently stir in the crab, then cover. Slip it into the oven and bake until the rice is tender and the liquid has been mostly absorbed, about 55 minutes. You'll need to check occasionally to make sure the pilaf hasn't dried out before the rice is tender. If so, stir in a little more broth, maybe ¼ cup, then cover and continue cooking. Let stand, covered, at room temperature for 5 to 10 minutes so the grains can relax and reabsorb some liquid, making them fluffier and more toothsome just before you scoop it up by the spoonful.

RINSE RAW RICE UNTIL THE WATER RUNS CLEAR.

DO YOU ALSO FLOSS YOUR CAT?

There was a time when rice was coated in talc, mostly to help it stay dry, like putting a little talcum powder in your sneakers on a hot day.

In fact, a few varieties of packaged rice are still coated in talc, mostly to survive the long voyage in container ships. But even these are ridiculous rarities, most of them slipped past various port inspections. So if you're buying the cheapest, bottom-of-the-barrel rice, these grains do need to be put in a fine-mesh sieve and rinsed thoroughly. The water will never run clear, but give it a go anyway. Or just buy better quality rice. Mostly because no amount of rinsing will get rid of all the talc.

That's not the only reason some people rinse rice, though. There are also a few health concerns.

If you're buying rice in bulk, it's not a bad idea to give it a rinse. You have no idea how many hands have been in the bin—or where those hands have been. That said, cold tap water will not kill bad bacteria. A few might go down the drain; others will stick around. That's why we prefer to buy rice in sealed bags.

If you're buying organic, local, right-from-the-farm rice, you might want to give the grains a rinse so you can pick through for any stones or pebbles that could clash with your butter sauce as well as your expensive orthodontia.

Some people rinse certain long-grain rices for pitch-perfect aesthetics. Varieties like jasmine or basmati are supposed to be dry and fluffy, not a single grain sticking to another. By rinsing them, these cooks are trying to remove some of the exterior starch that might cause clumping.

But the rationale here is a bit doubtful. Modern long-grain rice has been polished to an extreme degree, little starch left on the outside. Plus, new hybrids have been engineered to have the fewest sticky starches possible. So rinsing these is pretty much a throwback to old times.

In fact, you shouldn't rinse most varietals. Rice is a starch. No amount of rinsing will ever get rid of its even mildly sticky nature without ruining it. You'd need to wear the grains down to nothingness. Besides, you want a little sticky starch . . .

☞ so the grains will hold sauces on the plate, much as pasta does.

☞ so they'll pick up and carry flavors in a fried rice recipe.

☞ so that excess starch will slightly thicken a deep braise or stew in the bottom of a serving bowl.

Finally, a word about presoaking raw rice: it can cut the cooking time by as much as half. But it can also lead to mushy grains. Yes, a few rare varietals require presoaking, especially the very sticky ones used in Southeast Asian desserts. But really, there's no need to do it for almost all modern varietals. And besides, any time you've ostensibly saved, you've spent soaking rice!

AT HIGH ALTITUDES, INCREASE THE STATED OVEN TEMPERATURE BY 25°F.

CONTRARY TO POPULAR BELIEF, NO.

First off, temperature is not affected by altitude. A properly calibrated, preheated 350°F oven at sea level in Charleston, South Carolina, will be a properly calibrated, preheated 350°F one in Cheyenne, Wyoming.

However, at higher elevations, everything in the oven dries out more quickly. So if you *raise* the oven's temperature, you exacerbate the very problem caused by higher elevations.

Instead, make any adjustments in the moisture content of the recipes for both baking and roasting, as well as adjustments in the leavening for baking alone.

Let's turn to baking first, since it's the more complicated problem. Even at three thousand feet above sea level, the moisture in a batter or dough turns to gas bubbles more quickly, thanks to the lower boiling points of the various liquids in the mix.

Problem is, those bubbles can burst and escape before the internal structure of the cake is in place or the top is set—thereby resulting in a much drier, less satisfactory, perhaps flatter cake.

People advocate for the slightly higher oven temperature because it can help the batter's structure set more quickly. But it can also cause the top of the cake to burn. So the trade-off is not worth it. Besides, there are better ways to fix the problem.

Add a tablespoon or two of additional, beaten egg or milk to the mix, as well as a little extra flour for protein structure. Also, reducing the sugar and fat by small amounts (a tablespoon, for example) can also help set the structure more quickly. Both sugar and fat act as liquefiers in batters—and thus should be adjusted in high-altitude baking.

Over three thousand feet, you have to do all of the above—*plus* reduce the leavening. The bubbles will be coming faster and more often as the liquid comes to a boil even more quickly. Too much leavening and the batter will soufflé in the oven!

But once again, a higher baking temperature is not warranted. What's more, it does little for crisp baked items such as cookies—and, in fact, may cause them to spread more rapidly, singeing at the edges while staying raw at their centers.

That's all for baking; now let's go on to roasting. You'll just dry out the meat if you raise the oven's temperature. Instead, realize that it will take more time to get to the right internal temperature of the cut. So roast the meat covered half the time to keep its natural moisture intact. Baste it often thereafter. In other words, do anything and everything you can to keep moisture in and on the meat.

In the end, consider temperature your constant. Everything else—moisture, leavening, fat, and sugar—are the variables.

For more information, there are many excellent cookbooks on the market right now. Check out Susan Purdy's *Pie in the Sky* for an extraordinarily detailed set of solutions. And there's plenty of information available on the USDA's website.

4

GRILLING IS MAN'S WORK
Myths Told Before an Open Fire

Here's one that's puzzled us for years: a he-man who would never dream of cooking in the kitchen will heat up a grill, no problem. It's a fire, some meat, a few veggies. Does the open flame makes it man's work? Or caveman's work? Buddy, whether it's done in the kitchen or the backyard, it's still cooking.

Maybe this gender-identity riddle is what's given rise to some of these grilling myths. And if not, we're here to debunk them anyway.

THERE'S A DIFFERENCE BETWEEN GRILLING AND BARBECUING.

IF NO ONE UNDERSTANDS YOU, YOU'RE STILL NOT AN ARTIST.

We're about to offend every barbecue guru out there. But somebody's got to do it.

In the not-so-distant-but-simpler past, people went about their outdoor cooking without undo fussiness. When June Cleaver asked if Ward had fired up the barbecue, he didn't react in horror and say, "It's a grill, woman!"

In fact, nobody seemed to bother with the distinction between these words for years. A quick survey of cookbooks and food articles written before about 1985 reveals a surprisingly lax attitude to what today would be considered willful ignorance. In fact, they use the terms interchangeably, sometime within the same recipe.

Even now, the Hearth, Patio, and Barbecue Association makes no distinction between "grilling" and "barbecuing."

So what's with all the hairsplitting? Around the early '90s, a bunch of culinary grammarians invented a distinction which might—*might*—be useful in some circumstances. But more important, they invented a distinction to make themselves look smart and the rest of us dopey, as if we don't know what in the heck we're doing over that open fire.

They claim that grilling happens when you cook directly over the heat, the food searing on the grate right over glowing coals or flaming gas ranks. Barbecuing, on the other hand, takes place when you make use of indirect heat, the food to the side of said coals or gas ranks, the grill itself a big oven and the heat source not directly involved with the fare on the grate.

We'll give the culinary grammarians this: there's a big difference between cooking over direct heat and indirect heat. You certainly don't want to put a brisket over direct heat. The thing will be a piece of charcoal long before it's done. If you think brittle means tender, by all means incinerate that hunk of beef. Otherwise, it has to be cooked to the side of low heat for a very long time, the better to let the interstitial collagen melt and the whole thing turn gorgeously juicy.

And although you might cook salmon fillets or chicken breasts indirectly—that is, to the side of the heat—it'll take longer and requires extra fandango to get the grill ready. There's really no reason to spend all that extra time and energy when these simpler things benefit from the char that direct heat can give.

So yes, there's a distinction in the cooking methods—and it's important. But it's the technique that matters, not the diction. If we invite you over for a barbecue this weekend, you might get a perfectly grilled steak. If you want to turn up your nose and walk out based on a made-up linguistic quibble—*You said we were going to have barbecue!*—we'll be happy to clean your plate for you. Just leave the wine you brought on the table before you go.

MARINADES TENDERIZE MEAT.

SOMEBODY'S REALITY CHECK BOUNCED.

Marinades *flavor* meat—and only under some circumstances. They do little for its overall tenderness. To explain, we're going to have to break this down into the two marinade camps.

☞ *The sour ones.*

These contain an acid of some sort: wine, lemon juice, or vinegar, for example. They are said to break down the meat's fibers, rendering the cut more tender.

Yes and no. Sour marinades *do* break down fibers: cells collapse and pack in more tightly. But more tender? No. Packed-in cells mean tougher meat.

Think ceviche. Put raw fish in lime juice, let it be, and the fish gets firmer, not softer.

That said, some densely structured cuts—think flank steak or pork loin—can survive a sour marinade. Their cells are already tightly serried. Any collapsing is minimal. The real way these cuts get tender happens after they've been cooked— that is, with the slicing technique. Paper thin strips will be tender; hunks will be shoe leather.

But you say you've made a sour marinade work with, oh, a brisket. You probably set the meat in it, but then cooked the cut the same way you would have cooked it without said marinade—that is, a fairly low heat over a long time. It wasn't the marinade that tenderized the brisket; it was the cooking method.

However, the marinade did add flavor. But only *some*. Mostly to the outer surface. All sour marinades move slowly through meat, no more than a millimeter or so an hour. Put the marinated meat in the fridge and the protein structures tighten down, the marinade moving in even more slowly.

The best compromise? Use a low-acid, high-flavor marinade; the acid will worm its way in somewhat, bringing other flavors in tow. But then cook the cut in whatever way makes it tender: hot and fast for strip steaks or low and long for chuck roasts.

☞ **The sweet ones.**

These are made from various fruits, rhizomes, and vegetables, such as papayas, kiwis, pineapples, figs, and honeydew melons. All contain protein-busting enzymes that tenderize meat by digesting it. It's tender the way that pudding is tender. Even a short stay in these enzymes can render a cut mushy.

What's worse, these marinades don't carry flavors well at all. *And* many of these hungry enzymes are destroyed by heat. Bromelaine, the enzyme in pineapples, is such. Which is why *canned* pineapple makes no proper marinade at all.

Okay, now we know what partially works and what doesn't work. But there is one naturally occurring enzyme in beef that is itself a potential tenderizer: the sulfhydryl enzyme, which goes to work when the meat is aged, thus rendering the cut more tender.

The sulfhydryl enzyme works best in the presence of free calcium ions. Butchers and meat processors inject meat with calcium chloride to get the stuff moving. But since most of us don't have calcium chloride around the kitchen, we can find an easier, more palatable option: low-acid dairy products such as buttermilk or yogurt, as in tandoori marinades. These work a little better than those low-acid, high-flavor, sour marinades—although you can't let a cut of beef sit in a dairy marinade for more than a couple of hours because of the potential for bacterial overload. So the effect is compromised for safety's sake.

In the end, you can't trade in your steak knife for a bottle of marinade.

GRILLED LAMB CHOPS WITH CHERRY CHIPOTLE MARINADE

Makes 8 chops

We've talked about all the problems with marinades—and some of the solutions. We've got a little acid in this one (the vinegar) to keep the flavors moving. But more important, there's some good sweetness in that cherry jam. Thus, we have a marinade that gloms onto the surface of the meat and caramelizes over the heat.

It doesn't render the chops more tender, just way more flavorful. Which is the whole point with a simple dinner like this one. Works well on pork chops, too.

¼ cup cherry jam
1 canned chipotle in adobo sauce,
    stemmed, seeded, and minced
2 tablespoons red wine vinegar
¼ teaspoon salt
8 lamb loin or rib chops, about 1 pound

1. Stir the jam, chipotle, vinegar, and salt in a small bowl. Note: 1 *canned* chipotle, not 1 can of chipotles. Make that mistake and you'll be chewing on sticks of butter all night to try to get the capsaicin out of your mouth (see page 160).

2. Smear this mixture all over the lamb chops, set them in a big baking dish, cover, and refrigerate for at least 2 hours but not more than 4 hours.

3. Fire up the grill. Either heat a charcoal grill to high heat (about 500°F) for direct cooking or build a high-heat, nicely ashed coal bed in a charcoal grill, right under the grate. In either case, consider giving the grate a spritz with nonstick spray *before* you fire the thing up. If your grate is good and seasoned, there's probably no need. But never fire that can of aerosol oil into an open fire!

4. It's best if you take the chops out of the fridge while the grill heats up, about 15 minutes. Too cold and the meat can sear and even burn before the insides are done.

5. Set the chops directly over the heat, cover the grill, and cook for about 4 minutes per side, turning once, until an instant-read meat thermometer inserted into the thickest center of one of the chops registers 145°F. Note that we don't want the same temperatures as for beef. We're going with the USDA here—a little pink to the chops but not much, mostly for safety.

If you don't want to go to the hassle of using the grill, you can also broil the chops. Set the rack about 4 inches from the broiler element and preheat it for a good 10 minutes. Set the chops on a lipped baking sheet and place them under the broiler, trying to line them up with the element's heating ranks. They'll take about 3 minutes per side, turning once, in this hotter inferno; but as always, use an instant-read meat thermometer for the best results.

DON'T SALT MEAT BEFORE COOKING IT.

EXPERTS DISAGREE— FOR GOOD REASONS.

Everybody's got an opinion. Salt the meat right before cooking it. Salt it the day before. Don't salt it until you eat it.

One thing's true: salt does desiccate meat. A little. *A very* little. Not really enough to matter. Maybe if you buried that hunk of beef in a salt mound and left it there for a hundred years, by then it would be completely dried out. But so would you.

Yes, salt desiccates the outer, cellular layers of a piece of meat. But salt is also *hydrophilic*. It loves water. Attracts it. Thus, your ankles swell after Chinese food.

If you still believe that salt dries out meat and renders it inedible, we have two words for you: *kosher chicken*. To kosher a bird, you rub it in salt and let it sit. The salt brings water into the cells, keeps the moisture stable, and renders the bird ridiculously succulent.

Salt binds with surface moisture, forms a brine, and reenters the meat because of the shift in osmotic pressure among the cells.

So when *should* you salt the meat? That's another matter entirely.

Some chefs prefer salting it up to a day in advance, particularly chicken, turkey, and beef. They like the way the salt develops more complex flavors in the meat.

Others like to salt it just before it hits the heat. They like the crust the salt itself can form. (This is Bruce's preferred method.)

The difference is a matter of taste. The earlier salting will yield a more aged, complex flavor in the meat as the salt permeates down through the cell layers (about an inch a day if your fridge is set at 45°F). But the last-minute salting, right before the cut hits the fire, will yield a brighter, cleaner taste as the surface sugars break down, dissolve, mingle with the salt, and form a caramelized crust.

That doesn't mean you shouldn't also consider a little salt at the table, particularly high-end, gourmet sea salts. These are full of complex mineral profiles, many beyond the table-salt norm. These salts are a condiment, a garnish of sophisticated flavors that are bright and fresh with every bite.

GRILLED PRIME RIB

Around 8 servings

For this holiday or dinner party favorite, ask for bones 1 through 3, if possible—that is, the bones closest to the loin, farthest from the shoulder. These bones have the best meat, less fat in big blobs throughout. Do not let the butcher cut the meat off the bones and tie it back on. The whole point is to roast the flavor of the bones into the meat.

1 tablespoon coarse salt, such as kosher salt or coarse
  sea salt
1 tablespoon mild paprika
1 tablespoon freshly ground black pepper,
  even black peppercorns finely crushed
  with the bottom of a heavy skillet
One 3-bone, 6- to 7-pound standing rib roast,
  the meat still attached to the bones

1. Mix the salt, paprika, and pepper in a small bowl. Massage this evenly over the entire roast, even among the bones. Set aside while you heat the grill.

2. You'll need to prepare the grill for both direct and indirect cooking. For a gas grill, heat some of the ranks— perhaps half—for high-heat cooking, thereby leaving half the grill grate without a flame directly under it. For a charcoal grill, build a high-heat, well-ashed charcoal bed in the center of the grill, then use a grill rake to push the coals to the periphery of their grate. You'll also need extra charcoal briquettes to feed the fire.

3. Wrap the beef in heavy-duty aluminum foil, then set it in a large roasting pan or a disposable aluminum roasting pan. Set this pan with the roast in it on the *unheated* section of the grill grate, not directly over any fire. Cover the grill and roast until an instant-read meat thermometer inserted into the center of the meat without touching bone registers 110°F, about 1½ hours.

You'll note two problems. One: you need to monitor the heat, adjusting the gas levels or adding more briquettes so you're cooking at high heat, about 500°F, maybe a little higher.

And two: you have to unwrap that big piece of beef to take its internal temperature. Those juices inside are hot. Be very careful. Seal it up to continue cooking.

4. When the internal temperature is 110°F, unwrap the roast. The meat will be fairly gray (and unappetizing). Set that roast directly over the heat, on the section of the grill with the fire below it. Discard the pan, the foil, and all the (hot!) juices inside (mostly melted fat, of course). Continue cooking, turning the beef with big tongs and spatulas, until all sides are flame-licked and crunchy brown and an instant-read meat thermometer inserted into the center of the meat without its touching bone registers 125°F for rare (about 8 more minutes), 130°F for medium-rare (about 10 minutes), or 140°F for medium (about 15 minutes). Remember: timing is no guide; go by temperature.

5. Transfer the roast to a carving board or platter and let it stand at room temperature for 10 minutes, so that the meat fibers relax and juices reincorporate among them.

6. To carve the roast, position it on the board so the bones are pointing straight up and oriented to the right for a right-handed person or to the left for a left-handed person. Hold the roast in place with a meat fork. Use a thin carving knife to slice along and around the inside arc of the bones, thereby removing the center eye in one piece. Stand the eye cut side down on the carving board, hold it in place with a meat fork, and slice down, starting with one of the ends to create a thin slice and then carving off more as you move along the roast. We prefer steaklike, $\frac{1}{2}$-inch-thick slices. Finally, slice between the bones to separate them.

SOAK BAMBOO SKEWERS TO KEEP THEM FROM BURNING UP ON THE GRILL.

DEPENDS . . .

We tested this one several times, just to make sure. We used soaked and unsoaked skewers for shrimp, satay, chicken sausage halves, and kebabs made with beef cubes—all over medium heat on the grill.

The result: all the skewers burned.

To be sure, the soaked skewers didn't char as badly during the first two or three minutes of grilling—which means the shrimp and satay were done before the skewers incinerated. But their skewers were still blackened.

After two or three minutes, the unsoaked ones were also blackened. But they, too, were in no danger of falling apart.

So soaked or unsoaked, it didn't make an appreciable difference for the quick-cooking set—except for the more complicated matter of aesthetics. Yes, the soaked ones were slightly less carbonized, so they did look a tad better. But both soaked and unsoaked were holding their shape.

The real problem came with the long cookers, the chicken sausages and beef kebabs. Here, true to form, the dry skewers were more blackened after three minutes. But soon enough, even the soaked ones began to burn. And by the time the sausage halves and beef cubes were cooked through, even the soaked ones were good and charred, falling apart at their extremities, partly because of flare-ups. Soaked or unsoaked, both were desiccated.

One more thing: we were working on a gas grill with the flame hidden under metal slats. If we had been working on a charcoal grill with an open flame, the skewers would have been truly incinerated, no matter how much soaking we did.

Here's the truth: if the food cooks quickly, in at most three minutes, feel free to soak bamboo skewers if you want slightly less blackening at their tips. But if the food is to cook for more than three or four minutes, even ten minutes, especially over high heat, feel free to forgo the soaking. It won't make any difference.

If the blackened bits bother you, buy metal skewers. But remember: they'll cook the food more quickly because they'll heat from the inside as well as the outside. You'll need to shear 10 to 20 percent off the stated cooking time. But they'll need no soaking *and* you'll have great aesthetics. A win-win, for sure.

DON'T POKE THE MEAT OR ALL THE JUICES WILL RUN OUT.

LIFE IS NOT AN "ALL OR NOTHING" AFFAIR.

Yes, *some* of the juices will run out when you poke meat while it's cooking. When we tested this myth on the grill, we measured a little over ½ teaspoon of juices from a hole in a chicken thigh attached to the whole bird, a little under ½ teaspoon from a rib roast, and less than ¼ teaspoon from a one-inch-thick pork chop. In each case, those are just a smidgen of all the juices in the hunks of meat. So *all* the juices didn't run out; a tiny bit did.

We think this myth ultimately arose from fear of meat. You see a sweating hunk sitting on the cutting board and think, *Holy cripes, I'm going to ruin that. And I paid a fortune for it!*

Don't be nervous. A piece of meat is made up of billions of cells. And the fibers contain as many minuscule pockets of moisture as they have cells, not to mention all the stuff between the fibers, the fat and collagen, made up of their own cells, all of which also melt and create "juices."

Yes, when you poke a piece of meat, you inevitably rupture a handful of these cells—a.k.a. pockets of moisture. But it's a handful among legions.

Think about it like this: you grill a bratwurst. It eventually splits open. Juices run out, the flames spring up, and the whole thing gets irresistible. You bite into it and it's still luscious. So yes, you've lost some juices, but they are a mere drop in the ocean of fat sloshing around in that brat.

But no, you don't want to stab a piece of meat repeatedly over the heat. Don't take out your marital frustrations on your dinner. Follow the lead of your parents and take them out *during* dinner.

In truth, freezing and thawing a piece of meat ruptures far more cells than a poke with a meat fork. So perhaps you should worry less about poking it and more about its freshness.

And you can still dry out a piece of meat. You can cook it so long that its cells lose a ton of their moisture, the interstitial fat melts and flows away, even the collagen evaporates in the fiery furnace, holes or no holes from a meat fork. It's dry. Not because you poked it but because you overcooked it.

And that's because you didn't use an instant-read meat thermometer—which (yes!) pokes a hole in the meat when you probe it to make sure it's at the right temperature to be a juicy and wonderful dinner.

5

FLIGHTLESS WE SOAR
Myths About Our Fine-Feathered Friends

Birds make their appearances on our tables at major holidays. And yet, although we all know turkeys do the heavy lifting at Thanksgiving, most glossy food magazines like to pretend that Christmas is the time for ham or beef. Still, statistics show that most North Americans have a bird on the table for that holiday, too. And New Year's as well. Not to mention Rosh Hashanah and Passover.

In fact, there are few more iconic meals than a roast chicken or turkey, a staple of Sunday and Shabbat dinners. A bird often gets mixed up in people's memories of "grandmother's cooking."

Given the cultural provenance of our fine-feathered friends, it's hardly surprising that they come in for their fair share of long-lasting, culinary taradiddles. Here are the most stubborn.

YOU CAN THAW A CHICKEN OVERNIGHT IN THE REFRIGERATOR.

DO YOU ALSO HAVE A DESIGNATED TIME TO HUMILIATE YOURSELF IN PUBLIC?

No matter how many recipes proclaim that a five-pound bird will thaw in the fridge in twenty-four hours, it ain't gonna happen. It takes at least two full days, probably two and a half, if not a little longer, based on how cold you freezer is, how cold your refrigerator is, how much the bird weighs, and how high its meat-to-bone ratio is, a ratio that's been rising over the years with modern breeding practices that favor large-breasted, big-thighed, heavily muscled birds over their scrawnier, bonier progenitors.

If you've got nothing but time (and chicken) on your hands, here's the standard way to thaw a frozen bird: place it still in its packaging on a large plate to catch any drips and store it in the refrigerator for up to 3 days, depending on our stated factors. Unwrap the chicken when thawed so that it doesn't sit in its juices, set it back on a plate, refrigerate it uncovered, and cook it within 24 hours.

If you're more pressed for time, you can still roast a frozen chicken tonight—provided you start several hours in advance. Leave the frozen bird in its original packaging and submerge the whole thing in an enormous bowl of cool tap water. (Not warm. That can result in bacterial ickiness.) If the frozen bird's not in its original package, first seal it in a large, zip-closed bag, then do the immersing trick.

Clear the milk cartons and juice boxes out of your fridge. You'll need lots of room to store that huge bowl filled with water and a chicken. Until the bird is fully thawed, change the water every thirty minutes, swapping it out for more cool tap water.

Why all this to-do? The chicken is quite frigid from your freezer (which is probably set around 0°F); you need to keep immersing that bird in water that's cool but not as cold as your refrigerator (probably set around 40°F), so that the bird slowly warms up and thaws without bacterial overload. A three-pound broiler will take 3 hours in this immersion method. That means you need to change the water five times. A five-pound roaster, about 4½ hours. That's eight times.

When the bird is ready to roast, remember to dig the giblet packages out from the body cavity. Check both ends. Those innards can lurk anywhere.

In short, there's no shortcut to roast chicken. Except the rotisserie birds at the supermarket. If you're really in a rush and have a hankering for roast chicken tonight, get one of those.

PERFECT ROAST CHICKEN

It'll feed 4, maybe 6

This one's done in the classic French bistro style: crisp, brown, fantastic. And yes, buttered. The preparation gives the skin a ridiculous glaze, golden and decadent. If you'd rather not, you can always substitute olive oil, a lighter finish but no less delicious.

One 4-pound whole chicken, all the giblets
*   and neck removed*
Butchers' twine
3 tablespoons unsalted butter, at room temperature
*   (because you're not baking with it)*
1 tablespoon minced tarragon leaves
2 teaspoons stemmed thyme leaves
2 teaspoons Dijon mustard
1 teaspoon salt
½ teaspoon freshly ground black pepper

1. First, check the fit of the chicken in its roasting pan in your oven. You need at least three inches of head space between the chicken and the top of your oven. Position the rack as close to the center of the oven as you can to get the required space, if not more. Now preheat the oven to 375°F.

2. Next, you'll need to truss the bird with the butchers' twine, a dye-free, food-safe twine sold at most hardware stores and all cookware stores. Why? Roasting flattens meat because the fibers collapse. So to assure even cooking, you need to tie the bird so that it will hold its shape. Pull the wings up close to the breast to protect the white meat, then tie them in place by wrapping the twine around the bird a couple of times before knotting it. Also tie the legs together over the large opening, crossing them over each other and winding the twine around them before knotting it, thereby mostly closing the large opening.

Do not wash the bird. Contaminants are not killed with water but rather by heat. Work in the sink so you can bleach it out later. But don't bother rinsing down that bird. Little droplets of contaminated water can spray across your counters.

3. In a small bowl, mash the butter, tarragon, thyme, mustard, salt, and pepper until creamy. Spread this butter paste over the outside of the bird. There's only one way to do this: with your fingers. Get messy!

4. Set a rack in a large roasting pan, preferably an X-shaped chicken roasting rack, although any metal one will do so long as the bird is lifted off the pan's bottom. Set the bird in or on the rack breast side down—that is, the meatier, more rounded part down. Roast for 30 minutes.

5. Now for the tricky part. Turn the bird over. It's already hot. You might want to use silicone baking mitts. Or a large spatula and a pair of long-handled tongs. Or stick a long wooden spoon into the large opening, pick the bird up, and spin it around. Somehow, get it flipped so its breast is facing up without hot juices pouring all over you.

6. Continue roasting breast side up, basting often with the pan juices, until an instant-read meat thermometer inserted into the thickest part of the thigh as well as the breast registers 165°F without the probe's touching bone, about 45 more minutes. Remove the pan from the oven and set the bird aside, still on its rack in the roasting pan, for 10 minutes.

7. Transfer the bird to a carving board. While carving techniques vary, the easiest way to deal with a hot bird is to use kitchen shears—these can cut the thing into two wings, two legs, two thighs, and then the larger breast in half, after having snipped off the back. Don't wait a minute more. Get to the table and prepare for a feast.

MYTH #41

YOU HAVE TO THAW A TURKEY BEFORE ROASTING IT.

NOT TRUE!

Welcome to your worst nightmare. It's Thanksgiving morning, your mother-in-law is an hour away, and you realize the turkey is still in the freezer!

As we said for chicken, thawing a bird takes time. Lots of time. About four days for a twelve-pound turkey in a 40°F fridge. You should have started on the Sunday before the holiday. But you were too busy getting ready for your in-laws: painting the guest room, shampooing the carpets, and drinking your way through the liquor cabinet.

At this point, you've got two options:

1. Thaw the turkey in cool water.

Just as we did with the frozen chicken, fill an enormous bowl with cool tap water, submerge the still-packaged frozen turkey in it, and set that whole, nine-thousand-pound contraption in the fridge for about 8 hours, changing the cool water every thirty minutes.

Your mother-in-law surely won't notice that you're hauling a big bowl of turkey water to the sink every half hour. Or ask her to help. Those early years in Estonia probably made her stronger than you.

☞ *2. Just shove the frozen bird in the oven.*

You can't do this for smaller birds, but you sure can for turkeys! In fact, a frozen turkey roasts more evenly than a thawed one. Unwrap it and chip the frozen giblet packets and long neck out of the front and/or back cavities (check both), set the bird on the roasting rack in a large roasting pan, and heat the oven to 325°F. You can also run cool water into the bird to loosen the ice-crusted giblet packets, but they may be so sealed to the inner cavities that you'll leave too many bits of paper behind as you try to chip them out. In that case, check the bird after it's been in the oven about 45 minutes to see if they're unstuck. (They're already hot, so remove them with tongs.)

Roast that twelve-pound turkey until an instant-read meat thermometer inserted into the flesh of the thigh without touching bone registers 165°F, 5 to 7 hours. Especially since you're going the frozen route, also look for the same temperature in the thickest part of the breast—for safety's sake. If the bird starts to brown too darkly in the heat, tent it loosely with foil until the last thirty minutes or so.

Why the two-hour time range for roasting? Because not all freezers are set to the same temperature, so not all frozen turkeys start out at the same temperature. And not all turkeys have the same depth of meat on the bone. With a twelve-pounder, start checking at about the four-hour mark to tell where you stand.

And there's an added bonus to roasting a frozen turkey: it's far less likely to drip gunky juices around your kitchen, juices that can pose contamination problems on exposed surfaces.

But there's also one problem: you can't stuff a frozen turkey. But you can buy frozen stuffed turkeys. These should not be thawed. Unwrap the frozen stuffed bird and hold the cavity openings under running water until you can remove the giblet and neck packets which are sitting right at the opening. Then shove the still-frozen, still-stuffed bird in the oven and relax. There's absolutely no call for in-law-induced panic. You'll need to find another excuse to drink through the liquor cabinet.

EATING TURKEY MAKES YOU SLEEPY.

IF IT WERE ONLY THAT SIMPLE!

It's a good thing Norman Rockwell painted that iconic image of the turkey being set onto the table *before* everyone dug in. An hour later, he'd have found them all passed out.

By now, many of us have been taught to blame this sleep-inducing reaction on a lowly protein chain, an amino acid named *L-tryptophan*. Turkeys have it. We eat it. It's a precursor to a neurotransmitter called serotonin which has a calmative effect. Thus, we get sleepy.

Sounds simple, right? There are a few problems. Such as:

☞ 1. You have to ingest L-tryptophan on an empty stomach.

A really empty stomach. A growling, roiling, embarrassingly loud stomach. And if Aunt Bessie forced her broccoli dip on you before the meal, or if you had a bowl of soup for the first course, or even if you took a bite out of a dinner roll before you swallowed that first mouthful of turkey, you abrogated some of the soporific effect, if not all of it.

☞ **2. You have to ingest L-tryptophan without any other form of protein (a.k.a. any other amino acid).**

They all compete for space in your noggin. And they all counteract L-tryptophan's efficacy. And yes, there are many other amino acids in turkey. Meat's got a lot of protein in it, after all. If you really want to put everyone under the table, consider forming and roasting a vegetarian turkey of puréed kale and beets, laced with purified L-tryptophan. That'll do it.

☞ **3. You must consume a lot of L-tryptophan.**

Probably more than is in the whole bird. Even purified L-tryptophan is a *very* mild sedative. Do you get sleepy from eating soybeans—or the edamame in Japanese restaurants? They've got twice as much L-tryptophan as turkey. Or how about eggs? Ounce per ounce, they have four times as much.

Listen, it's not the turkey that makes you nod off. It's the sheer volume of food, much of it carb heavy: the sweet potato casserole, the homemade rolls, the pie. And how many glasses of wine did you have, hmm? Your insulin levels are whacked.

What's more, you have to work to digest all that food. It's like putting your stomach on a treadmill for an hour or two. Let's face it: eating wears you out.

And then there's what passes for conversation in your family. How many times can your Aunt Bessie tell you about her date with the Kaiser? It doesn't matter if he was a lively dancer. That story would put anyone to sleep.

MYTH #43

WHITE MEAT CHICKEN IS HEALTHIER THAN DARK MEAT.

SO MARGINALLY TRUE AS TO BE MEANINGLESS.

A hundred thousand sandwich commercials can't be wrong. White meat chicken has got to be healthier than dark. They wouldn't lie, would they? Just to sell sandwiches?

In fact, the white meat craze is so white hot that the United States government has been forced to spend a cool $14 million to buy up dark meat chicken currently lying useless in cold storage. The meat is going to nutrition assistance programs, but it just goes to show you how nuts we are for the white stuff.

We might want to reconsider. The truth is more nuanced—as always.

It's true that white meat chicken is lower in calories and fat than dark meat—but not by much. By about 10 calories per ounce and 1 gram of fat, depending on the bird itself. If you eat half a chicken, that difference can really add up. But if you eat a standard portion, we're not talking a revolutionary difference.

What's more, the dark meat has lots of nutrients that the white meat lacks: more iron, more zinc, more B_6 and B_{12} vitamins.

And then there's the central problem with white meat: its utter tastelessness. Most of it ends up as boneless skinless chicken breasts. God save us. They're prone to sharding when cooked a second longer than necessary and irredeemably ho-hum most of the time.

The only way to make white meat palatable is to eat it on the bone—and with the skin. And let's face it: the skin is the real culprit. Almost a quarter of the calories and a heaping portion of the fat in a piece of chicken come from its skin—which itself weighs significantly less than the heftier meat inside. If you really want to cut down on the calories and fat, you'll lose that crispy skin on either the breast or the thigh. But why bother? What's another few minutes on the treadmill?

In any event, don't eat the whole chicken. It's the portion size that'll do you in. A standard serving of chicken is four ounces. Many subs from delis and chain sandwich shops have at least twice that amount, much of it doped with salt, then cooked, ground, shellacked with more salt, injected with broth and chemical emulsifiers, formed, extruded, shaped into a football, and sliced at the counter.

So yes, if you want to sit down to a pound and a half of chicken, go for the white meat because you'll live marginally longer. (Say, a week.) But if you eat manageable portions, have some dark meat. It'll taste good—and with its nutrition profile, do you some good, too.

JERK CHICKEN THIGHS

This will feed 8 if you've got some side dishes.

Jerk is a Jamaican seasoning rub, a fruity, balanced blend that takes the fire of a five-alarm habañero and morphs it into a deeply flavored tingle. Here, you'll actually make the rub, rather than buy a bottled mix—and it doth take a spice cabinet. Don't be deterred. The difference is significant. And if you've got any questions about how to handle that chile, see page 160.

6 medium scallions, thinly sliced

1 habañero chile, stemmed, seeded, and quartered

1 medium garlic clove, quartered

2 tablespoons red wine vinegar

2 tablespoons peanut oil

1 tablespoon minced, peeled fresh ginger

1 tablespoon packed dark brown sugar

1 teaspoon dried thyme

1 teaspoon ground allspice

1 teaspoon ground cinnamon

1 teaspoon ground coriander

1 teaspoon salt

1 teaspoon freshly ground black pepper

4 pounds skinless, bone-in chicken thighs

1. Place the scallions, chile, garlic, vinegar, peanut oil, ginger, brown sugar, thyme, allspice, cinnamon, coriander, salt, and pepper in a food processor fitted with the chopping blade, a mini food processor, or a very large spice grinder (though you may need to finely chop the scallions to get them all inside). Process or grind until blended into a fairly smooth if a little grainy purée—certainly not baby food, but also no chunks left in the mix. (If you've used a spice grinder, you might have trouble getting lurking bits of capsaicin out of its interior. The best advice is to wipe it out with a damp paper towel, then repeatedly grind raw white rice in it, wiping the powder out each time and doing it again, thereby removing most if not all of the other spice and chile oils.)

2. Scrape and pour this jerk purée over the thighs in a big bowl. Stir well until all the thighs are evenly coated. Cover and refrigerate for at least 2 hours or up to 6 hours.

3. Position the rack in the center of the oven and preheat the oven to 375°F.

4. Pour the contents of that big bowl into a 9 x 13-inch baking dish. Be sure to scrape the residual marinade out of the bowl and sprinkle on top of the thighs. Cover the baking dish with a sheet of parchment paper, then a sheet of aluminum foil; seal it up tightly and roast for 30 minutes. (Why both parchment paper and foil? The foil does the actual work of sealing in the moisture, but it shouldn't touch acidic things like this marinade. Thus, the parchment paper barrier. Look for parchment paper near the foil at the supermarket.)

5. Uncover the baking dish and continue to roast until the thighs are tender and glazed, and an instant-read meat thermometer inserted into one registers at least 165°F, basting often and rearranging the thighs for even cooking. Cool for a few minutes before serving—perhaps over cooked white rice and wilted greens, like collards or chard.

CHICKENS IN THE WILD WOULD BE ALL DARK MEAT.

IF THIS SOUNDS REASONABLE, UP YOUR MEDICATION.

Once upon a time, the sky was filled with chickens. They swooped and swung in widening gyres, taking their place among the falcons, competing with the eagles for the rocky escarpments. Come autumn, the chickens would gather in large groups to migrate down to Miami where they would bask in the sun, enjoy the early-dinner specials, and complain about the cost of everything.

Um, no. You're more likely to see a chicken hitchhiking to Florida. Because chickens don't fly much. Neither do turkeys. They're ground birds. Not quite as landlocked as emus, but certainly more so than eagles and egrets.

How'd this myth ever get started? Someone probably once learned that dark meat chicken (or turkey) is in fact dark because it's mobile muscle, heavily used. Thus, the reasoning goes, if chickens were somehow not tied to the barnyard, their breasts would be in use, the muscles taut from flight; since we have locked them into coops, their breast muscles have turned white.

The real story is that chickens (and turkeys) have two different sets of muscles: fast-twitch fibers and slow-twitch ones. The breast is made up of the former. These fast-twitch fibers are stocked with glycogen, a sugar that provides short bursts of energy, and so are good for limited, quick movements—like flying up to a roost. On the down side, fast-twitch fibers tire quickly. Very quickly.

For endurance, you need slow-twitch fibers, the kind found in abundance in chicken legs and thighs. These muscles are stocked with myoglobin, a protein structure that is adept at storing oxygen for long, continuous movement; so they tire out far more slowly. Which is why a chicken can walk around all day and not complain about her feet.

That myoglobin stains the meat dark. As you can imagine, ducks and geese are almost 100 percent slow-twitch muscle because these fowl have to be in flight for incredibly long periods of time—and then paddle around a pond or waddle across a highway, backing up traffic into the next state. So much to do, so little time.

While we're on the subject, humans have both fast-twitch and slow-twitch fibers. In fact, we have more fast-twitch than slow-twitch—which is why most people are better at short, contained tasks like sitting down, rather than long endurance ones like running a marathon. That said, star athletes can actually increase the amount of slow-twitch muscle in their bodies over years of strenuous exertion.

So yes, the dark meat is more oxygenated. But the white meat would not turn dark were chickens flying free. Because chickens can't fly free—or for extended periods of time. They couldn't even if they wanted to because they have little to few slow-twitch muscle fibers in their breasts.

THE RED JUICE IN A PACKAGE OF CHICKEN IS BLOOD.

MILLY-VANILLY SOUNDED GOOD, TOO.

In the meat section in the supermarket, everything is precut and sealed under cellophane. You can almost convince yourself that what's in that package of chicken breasts didn't come from a living animal.

Almost. Until you see that red liquid sitting underneath the chicken breasts. Uh-oh. Does this mean that chicken comes from chickens? The horror!

We can set your mind at rest—at least partially. If the red stuff in the package were blood, it would coagulate. It doesn't. So it isn't.

Basically, it's illegal to sell meat with the blood still in it in the United States. So the blood is drained and removed at slaughter. This is all because of a long, complicated history of dietary laws, many of them based on religious traditions and many of them more squeamish on this side of the pond than the European common laws on which they were initially based. Anyway, no blood.

Or almost none. Yes, a tiny bit remains. A very tiny bit. And it stays in place inside the major muscle groups. It doesn't flow out into that package.

So what is that red liquid? It's myoglobin, the stuff that gives slow-twitch muscles their commanding power. Chicken—and all other animals, for that matter—are made up of high amounts of water. Some of that water does leak out when cells are cut, when the breasts, for example, are trimmed off the birds. The water then mixes with residual myoglobin in the muscle. The myoglobin oxidizes and turns red, thus staining the water pink.

So is it blood? No, but it does come from the animal. Not to sound callous, but if that information bothers you, there are plenty of other choices for your culinary adventures. Because the worst thing is to kid yourself that it wasn't once an animal. You then lose sight of how you're living your life. Not that we'd give up meat. We're confirmed omnivores. But we want to do everything with our eyes open. It works out better that way.

FREE-RANGE CHICKENS RANGE FREE.

MAYBE IN SOME SHANGRI-LA.

The first time your chicken dinner sees the outdoors may well be when you grill it. Free-range chicken, as defined by the USDA, means:

Producers must demonstrate to the agency that the poultry has been allowed access to the outside.

For those of you not proficient in bureaucrat-speak, let's break it down:

Must demonstrate. When? Once a day? Once a year? The guidelines don't specify.

Must demonstrate *how*? Also not specified.

Has been allowed access. How? Doesn't say. A two-by-two square door in one wall of an enormous barn, the size of an airplane hanger? Yep, that counts as *allowed access.*

The outside. Meaning a field full of grub worms and tall grasses, a paradise for chickens? Or a concrete slab? A five-by-five slab outside that two-by-two door? Doesn't say. Which means a chicken would have to find her way to the door and then want to go outside. If you've ever been to one of those giant poultry farms, you'd know that it stinks out there among the mounds of chicken poop. You'd stay inside, too.

Besides, supermarket chickens are none too good at walking. By and large, they are members of the *Cornish cross-broiler* family and have been selectively bred so they're perfectly shaped for the plucking machines. They hobble around. At best. They also have such Arnold Schwarzenegger–size chests that by the time they're seven weeks old, they can't walk upright, much less go outside to the concrete slab among the chicken poop mounds. Even if they wanted to.

Furthermore, there are currently no regular field inspections by the USDA. There are periodic inspections, mostly after the people unfortunate enough to live next door to one of those gigantic poultry factories report any cheats and abuses they see, in the hopes that said factory farm might just go away.

In the end, and most unfortunately for all of us, labeling these days doesn't tell us anything about how a chicken was raised. The facts of a chicken's hard-scrabble life on an industrial farm, even a farm that's allegedly a *free-range* sort of place, just don't line up with the public's nostalgia for chickens roaming free in tall grasses.

To become an informed consumer, know your producer. What breed of chicken is it? How was it raised? How did it live its life? What did it eat? A judicious, fifteen-minute Internet search will tell you everything you need to know.

And if it doesn't, you'll find plenty of honest-to-God, free-range chickens at your local farmers' market—where you can actually shake the hand of the person who supervised what went on in the chicken's short but (we hope) contented life among tall grasses.

COOKED CHICKEN THAT'S STILL PINK IS NOT SAFE TO EAT.

NOT REALLY.

As we've already stated, when cooking meat, color is no indicator of doneness. The only way to know if chicken is done is to take its temperature.

However, the required temperature for chicken is different from beef (see page 101). You're not looking for the moment when the juices run clear, or when the meat feels a certain way, or when the bird can no longer talk back. Instead, you're looking for the instant-read meat thermometer to read 165°F.

By the way, this temperature is a change from several years ago when the USDA had us incinerating birds to 170°F and even 180°F, a ridiculously overvigilant precaution for safety. Fortunately, we can now relax and enjoy juicier, better-tasting chicken.

To use that instant-read thermometer, insert the probe at an angle into the inner thigh, particularly the thick end that faces the large cavity opening, diagonaling the probe into the thickest part of the meat without its touching the bone. Hold it there for a couple of seconds until the temperature stabilizes.

But taking a *large* bird's temperature at the thigh is not sufficient. Also, check the deepest, thickest part of the breast. For very large turkeys, also check the inner bits of the drummette on the wing. Every part should read 165°F, not just the thigh.

Given all this information, we hereby propose a new constitutional amendment: *an instant-read meat thermometer shall be a right for all citizens.*

If only. . . . Ah well, temperature is still key. However, sometimes when chicken is cooked to 165°F, well past the kill point for salmonella and other bad pests, the meat remains pinkish, a rosy hue in the creamy white. Why?

☞ If there's remaining myoglobin in the meat, it can set into a heat-stable, pinkish caste.

☞ Smoking or grilling can exacerbate this reaction.

☞ Darkening around the bones can occur, particularly in young birds whose bones are not fully set. These bones then leach pigment-laced proteins from their marrow, staining the meat pink.

If you want your chicken juicy, you want it no more than 165°F as an internal temperature. In chef parlance, that's *bloody at the bone*—although it's not blood but marrow, pigment, and myoglobin, as we've said. Chef shorthand is not always accurate.

Don't worry. You're still safe. In France, they daringly eat pinkish chicken that is cooked to temperatures well below 165°F. Sometimes around 140°F.

And in Japan, they eat *torishimi*, sliced raw chicken, a sort of chicken sashimi. There's just no accounting for taste!

6

ATTACK OF THE KILLER TOMATOES
Myths from the Kingdom of the Plants

Somewhere deep down, most of us probably suspect that vegetarianism is the right way to go. Better for the planet, better for our hearts, better for our budgets—all the standard reasons. You may have had one of those youthful dalliances with it in college. Everybody was experimenting. With a lot of things. But senior year, you went to a party on someone's deck, got a whiff of the grill, fought a fierce battle of the wills with a burger, and were finally vanquished by those wily omnivores and their barbecuing ways.

As if to compensate for all that drama, the rest of us refuse to give fruits and veggies a second glance. We fuss over the main course for a holiday meal, a sweating hunk of meat, only pair it with a microwaved bag of green beans, the tang of plastic in the air.

What with being the subject of both angst and neglect, fruits and vegetables come in for their fair share of myths. Let's put to rest the biggest doozies.

MYTH #48

A CHILE'S BURN IS IN THE SEEDS.

NOT *IN* BUT *ON*—AND NOT ALWAYS.

A chile is a fruit. Like all fruits, it has seeds. And because it has seeds, it also has placenta, those white membranes that hold the seeds in place—and pack the heat. As the chile is jostled—shaken, picked, cut, and transported—little sacs of the hot stuff break open in the placenta and spray their chemical fire onto the seeds. This is the plant's way of defending its next generation from the enemy—that is, you and me. We have molars; we grind food; we turn seeds to pulp; the plant can't reproduce. "Burn 'em good," the chiles say.

By contrast, birds aren't bothered by the burn. They don't have molars. They swallow the seeds whole, don't really digest them, and, um, "broadcast" them far and wide. The plant can produce another generation. "Eat up, our fine-feathered friends," the chiles say.

The burn we—and all molared mammal pals—experience comes from a compound we've already met: capsaicin, a chemical found in all chiles, from ultramild bell peppers to sweet/sour jalapeños and sociopathic habañeros.

Capsaicin causes a burning sensation on mucus membranes—that is, on those bits right inside the body that have a slimy coating to protect them from what's bad just outside. Like capsaicin. Among other things.

When you're working with chiles, your fingers don't burn when they're coated in capsaicin. That's because there's no mucus membrane exposed—unless you have a cut or a puncture wound. The real victims are the insides of your mouth, the corners of your eyes, the inner bits of your ears, and other delicate parts not to be mentioned here.

Capsaicin doesn't burn the way fire or even acid does. Instead, it causes the *sensation* of burning. It binds to and rewires a neural receptor (VR1), allowing positive ions to fizz through the gap. This is the same depolarization that happens when a nerve is actually burned or abraded. Thus, capsaicin feels like a burn without actually being a burn.

Capsaicin also increases blood flow. Which is why your lips can turn red from a chile's burn. And also why capsaicin has been turned into a topical analgesic cream for sore muscles.

A cream—that's the key. Capsaicin is not water soluble. Drinking iced tea or beer or water or soda or wine will do nothing for the burn. If your beverage is cold, it may numb the area, but not for long.

To stop a chile's burn, lard it up. Capsaicin is fat soluble. So butter that tortilla.

Or nibble that hunk of Cheddar.

Or swig some whole milk.

Or polish off a bowl of whipped cream.

The same goes for any part of your body. To get capsaicin off your hands, pour a little oil into your palms; rub it around, even between your fingers; and then wash your hands thoroughly with soap and water.

Or plan ahead and wear rubber gloves in the first place.

PEELING A POTATO REMOVES THE VITAMINS.

LIFE'S RARELY THAT SIMPLE.

Although there's a lot of good flavor in a potato skin, you don't compromise the vitamins by peeling the thing. You do, however, compromise the fiber content.

A potato's skin is a protective coating that grows thick and crusty once the tuber has been pulled out of the ground. That skin contains half the fiber in a spud. And some of the potassium—although there's more in the spud itself. More than in most other fruits and vegetables. A medium potato has 720 mg of potassium; a large banana, 400 mg. Has your doctor told you to eat a banana because of heart issues? Try French fries!

So what's left in the potato without its fibrous skin? Plenty of iron, vitamin B6, niacin, folate, riboflavin, magnesium, manganese, phosphorus, and C—most of which is bunched in a vein just below the skin. If you peel that tuber with shallow cuts, you'll keep these nutrients intact.

Some people claim that if you boil potatoes with their skins on, they'll retain more vitamin C. In fact, they'll retain little. Vitamin C is destroyed by heat. It doesn't matter whether those spuds were wearing their jackets in the boil.

Unfortunately, there can be bad stuff on a spud *not* destroyed by heat. That is, the green stuff, a.k.a. solanine, a mild poison that develops as certain natural chemicals react to light.

Potatoes grow underground. They can become bitter and dangerous up here in the sunlight. Like your Cousin Myrtle when she's forced to go out in public.

Solanine can cause a host of yucky problems, including a bad case of the runs. But don't worry. You have to eat a lot of solanine. Like an enormous bowl of mashed potatoes made from *only* the green bits.

Still, it's best to avoid solanine. Store potatoes out of the light in a cool, dry, dark place—like the back corner of a pantry. The less light, the fewer green spots. Avoid the refrigerator, not because of increased solanine, but because the chill turns off certain flavor compounds that will never switch back on. Also, before cooking a potato, cut out any green spots, as well as any "eyes" that have sprouted.

And one more thing while we're clarifying myths about potatoes: new potatoes are not necessarily *new*. Yes, they *can* be early potatoes. But mostly, they're mature, small, red-skinned potatoes. Small doesn't mean young. We're back to your Cousin Myrtle.

So boil or steam those spuds, mash them, and enjoy them with or without their skins. Most of the nutrition—with the exception of the vitamin C—remains intact, despite being swamped with the two sticks of melted butter you just poured into the bowl.

PUTTING AN AVOCADO PIT IN THE GUACAMOLE WILL KEEP IT FROM TURNING BROWN.

IN YOUR DREAMS.

Avocados contain chemical compounds that fuse with oxygen and cause guacamole to turn brown. A mere pit can't stop the chemical onslaught.

Here's how the whole thing goes down: when you slice an avocado open, polyphenols are released from their storage chambers in the flesh. These polyphenols then combine with enzymes already in the fruit. The resulting compounds are exposed to oxygen in the air. Which causes them to morph further, the green turning a mucky brown as the final compounds absorb light. A pit in the mix may limit the oxygen exposure—but only directly underneath the pit!

In truth, that browning and muckifying are the plant's natural defenses at work. When a bug bites into an avocado, those same polyphenols are released to combat the digestive enzymes in the pest's mouth. And they work pretty well. A bug bite in the berry (yes, an avocado is a berry, not a fruit or vegetable) is brown at its margins but often doesn't turn into a big, mushy spot in the flesh—depending, of course, on how hungry that bug was and how virulent its enzymes were.

But there are no pest enzymes present when a knife slices into an avocado. Thus, the polyphenols look around for other enzymes to kick around. They find ones naturally occurring in the avocado itself. And so they start to pick a fight, this time against their own team. But it takes a while. Up to nine hours. Pit or no pit, that tempting bowl of fresh guacamole will likely be devoured long before it has a chance to brown.

Also, refrigeration helps. The polyphenols and enzymes devour their food more quickly when they're a little warm, like pensioners in Florida. A good chill keeps them hunkered down.

In addition, acids hamper the work of polyphenols. However, not all acids are created equal—which is why lime juice works better than balsamic vinegar. Lime (or lemon) juice is doped with ascorbic acid—a.k.a. vitamin C, which is an oxygen vacuum cleaner. It sucks it right out of the air—and out of the guacamole. That's why some manufacturers add purified ascorbic acid directly to their packaged guacamole. Voilà: less brown.

Of course, over time, even ascorbic acid loses its efficacy. The guacamole in the bowl starts to go gunky because, let's face it, there's more polyphenol oxidase in that big avocado than there is ascorbic acid in that little lime.

So let's review the solutions to browning guacamole:

1. **Don't make it ahead.**

2. **Keep it chilled.**

3. **Make sure there's a vitamin C-rich acid like lemon or lime juice in the mix.**

4. **Limit the guacamole's exposure to oxygen by putting plastic wrap right down on the surface.**

By the way, these steps work for pesto, too.

PERFECT GUACAMOLE

Serves 4

Despite the lack of variety at your local grocery store, there are many varieties of avocados, from the long, thin Pinkerton to the roundish, summery-sweet Reed. However, Hass avocados, the sturdy, good-for-transport, teardrop berries that turn dark green, even black as they ripen, are the ones that show up year-round. When you pick one up, it should be heavy to the hand and give when gently squeezed, neither firm nor mushy. Now it's perfect for guacamole. You can also ripen them by sealing them in a paper bag with an apple, which gives off ethylene gas, a ripening agent. They will get softer but not necessarily sweeter.

3 large ripe Hass avocados
2 medium garlic cloves
3 tablespoons lemon juice

½ teaspoon ground cumin
½ teaspoon salt
½ teaspoon freshly ground black pepper
Several dashes hot red pepper sauce,
    such as Tabasco sauce
2 cherry tomatoes, quartered
¼ cup minced red onion

1. First, peel and pit the avocados. Cut them length-wise around the seed, starting at the flatter bottom and working your knife around the whole berry. Rotate the halves and pull them apart. The pit will still adhere to one half. Use a flatware spoon to lift the pits out: gently pry the spoon under them and lift up. Discard the pits. Set the six halves cut side down on your cutting board. Beginning at the small end, peel off the skins with your fingers or a paring knife. Set aside two of the halves.

2. Place the remaining four halves in a serving bowl and mash them with the tongs of a fork, working the meat again and again through the tines until it turns into a soft if still somewhat coarse purée—no big chunks, but not wallpaper paste either. Another great tool for this task is a potato masher. You can really get it down in the bowl and work the green stuff into a pulpy purée.

3. Mash the garlic cloves through a garlic press and into the bowl. No press? Then mince them very fine. You can also use jarred, finely minced garlic, about 1 teaspoon, maybe a little more.

4. Stir in the lemon juice, ground cumin, salt, black pepper, and hot red pepper sauce. Again, a fork works best.

5. Now for the remaining avocado halves. Turn them over and dice them into small cubes. Stir these into the guacamole along with the quartered cherry tomatoes and the minced red onion. Either eat the guacamole now or smooth it out in the bowl, press plastic wrap against its surface, and refrigerate for several hours until you're ready to dive in.

NEVER PUT BANANAS IN THE FRIDGE.

"NEVER" IS SUCH AN UGLY WORD.

Will the quest for the six-week fruit never end? Fruit goes bad. No matter how much you want it to stick around, it goes mushy and eventually turns fizzy under the skin.

Fruits and vegetables rot. Mostly to expose their seeds. Which are fed by naturally occurring starches, themselves eventually liquefying into simpler sugars. That's called *nature*.

Yes, a good chill helps. With bananas, too. That banana on your counter was shipped in cold storage before making its way to you.

But still you want to save it. So you put it in the fridge—where the peel turns black. Why? Cold temperatures can cause certain ripening chemicals in the banana's peel to go into overdrive. It's probably a natural signal to the fruit that cooler weather is coming, so it's time to get off the tree, rot, and plant its seeds in the ground.

That said, the enzymes *inside* the fruit itself, the ones that break starches into sugars, don't go into overdrive just because of the chill. The fruit needs to stay good so its flesh can nourish the seeds. Thus, those internal enzymes hang back so the fruit inside the peel stops ripening.

To put it simply, at room temperature, the banana flesh gets softer more quickly but the peel stays more lightly colored; in the fridge, the banana peel gets darker more quickly but the flesh stays firmer longer. So if the banana is green, leave it out on the counter. Once it gets to the stage of ripeness you like, put it in the fridge.

For bananas from the store with no green but no brown spots either, figure on four days on the counter, maybe ten in the fridge. And if you really want to keep bananas around for a long time, peel them, cut them into three-inch sections, seal them in a plastic bag, and freeze them. They'll be great for smoothies, *blech* for most other things.

Last, at the risk of burying the lead, putting bananas in the fridge doesn't turn them poisonous either. That howler makes the occasional rounds as well, but nobody's ever dropped dead from bananas because they were cold. If cold bananas killed, then everyone would have dropped dead from eating banana cream pie or banana pudding or those hideous gelled salads with little bits of banana floating in them. Okay, maybe from that last one, but not the others.

PEANUTS ARE A NUT.

ONLY IF YOU TRUST A BUREAUCRAT.

Just because you call it *tinfoil* doesn't mean it's made of tin. And just because you call a peanut a *nut* doesn't mean it is one.

A nut is an indehiscent fruit. That is, *not opening at maturity.* Many fruits open up as they mature, exposing their seeds to the wind or the birds. Think wheat or rice. Or even overripe, rotting peaches on a tree. By contrast, a nut develops a protective, hard shell—actually its ovary—that can't be opened without effort. The flesh inside, what we actually eat, is both the fruit and its own seed all at once, not two separate things, as they are in, say, oranges with their orange pulp and white seeds.

Given all these distinctions, the most common nuts you're likely to find are chestnuts, hazelnuts, hickory nuts, pecans, and walnuts. Acorns, too, although the varieties from red oaks are so full of tannins, so very bitter, that they require boiling and processing to make them barely palatable. We'll leave them to the squirrels.

Now on to the peanut. It's not a fruit, a seed, or a nut. It's a legume.

Peanuts form when the pollinated flowers of the peanut plant bend over and insert themselves into the ground, so that the emerging legumes come to maturity down in the dark. The hulls are papery and fibrous, not hard (as with nuts). And what you eat—that is, the little seeds inside—are about like the seeds inside of any other bean, a soy bean or a pinto bean, even like the seeds inside a green bean.

Peanuts aren't the only ones that are not nuts:

- Brazil nuts, cashews, pistachios, and pine nuts are all seeds.

- Macadamia nuts are kernels, not nuts at all.

- Almonds are actually the seeds of drupes—that is, related to peaches, nectarines, and cherries.

- Coconuts are themselves drupes.

That said, the USDA sometimes lumps many of these together as *tree nuts*—including peanuts! This oversimplification is not so much a matter of bureaucratic laziness as it is about certain allergy-inducing compounds common among them. If your child has a tree nut allergy, he or she may or may not also have a peanut allergy. And this lumping together has to do with industry practice—peanuts make an appearance in a can of *mixed nuts*. Plus, it has to do with culinary history, which has mislabeled these things for centuries.

All of which has nothing to do with the botany of nuts.

AFRICAN GROUND NUT STEW

6 bowlfuls

Since peanuts are actually legumes, they can be cooked just like beans—and lend a pleasing, earthy flavor to soups and stews. This one's a version of Ma'afe, a traditional stew from Mali, said by some to help you get in touch with your ancestors. It probably comes from the fact that peanuts, a staple crop in Africa, come from underground, where your ancestors are supposed to live. In any case, these lovely legumes add lots of protein to this luscious vegetarian stew, deep and rich, the perfect thing for a chilly evening.

1½ cups unsalted roasted peanuts

1 cup water

2 tablespoons peanut oil

1 medium yellow onion, chopped

1 medium red bell pepper, cored, seeded, and chopped

4 medium garlic cloves, finely chopped

1 teaspoon salt

½ teaspoon cayenne

One 14-ounce can diced tomatoes, with their juice

1½ pounds sweet potatoes, peeled and cut into 1-inch cubes

1½ pounds yellow-fleshed potatoes, peeled and cut into 1-inch cubes

Up to 3 cups reduced-sodium canned vegetable broth

1 pound soft, leafy greens, such as chard, escarole, or spinach

1. Put the peanuts and water in a food processor fitted with the chopping blade. Pulse many times until you get a chunky, wet paste.

2. Heat a large pot over medium heat. Swirl in the oil, then add the onion and bell pepper. Cook, stirring often, until they soften and the onion begins to turn translucent, about 4 minutes.

3. Dump in the garlic, salt, and cayenne. Cook for 30 seconds. (Those chile oils can volatilize and burn your eyes. Stand back but stir occasionally.)

4. Stir in the canned tomatoes and all their juice. As the liquid comes up to a bubble, keep on stirring so that you release any burned bits from the bottom.

5. Stir in the sweet potatoes as well as the yellow-fleshed potatoes, then stir in all that coarse peanut purée. Bring to a simmer, stirring constantly, about 3 minutes.

6. Now add the broth. It's hard to know exactly how much. Basically, you want to pour in just enough to cover everything in the pot. Too much and the soup can be a little watery. But too little and things can stick. It's a trade-off—and you'll have to watch the pot, perhaps adding more broth as time goes on. Bring the whole thing to a simmer; then cover the pot, reduce the heat to low, and simmer slowly until the potatoes are tender when poked with a fork, 30 to 40 minutes, again adding more broth if you need it.

7. Meanwhile, cut the fibrous center stems out of the leafy greens. Wash the leaves under cool running water to remove any dirt and grit, then chop them without drying them.

(Note: Kale and collard greens would take a long time to cook over the heat. These other leafy greens go in at the last minute for a quick cook.)

8. Stir in the chopped greens, cover the pot, and continue simmering, stirring fairly frequently, just until the greens are tender, 10 minutes at most. Soup's on; dish it up.

NEVER SALT BEANS BEFORE YOU COOK THEM.

WHAT IS IT WITH PEOPLE AND THE WORD "NEVER"?

To salt or not to salt. That is the question. Whether 'tis nobler in the mind to suffer the pains and indigestion of outrageously insipid beans, or . . .

There are about as many myths about beans as there are about Shakespeare. Most of the myths about the Bard's life have been disproved, and we're here to do the same for our nutritious friend, the bean.

First, let's dispense with the whole salt/beans thing. Almost every can of beans is presalted. And the beans inside are not tough or bad or spoiled or ruined. They're silky and wonderful. So there's the end of that myth.

If you dump dried, unsoaked legumes in a pot and let them simmer over the heat, salting them as they cook is the right way to go. Dried beans won't become soup in ten minutes; they get tender at their own rate. Some take hours in a simmering broth. The salt then has a chance to meld with other flavors, suppressing bitter notes while enhancing sweet, sour, and umami ones. In other words, more taste per bite.

If you're the type who first soaks dried beans in water (and we're coming to this myth next), you *can* reduce the beans' cooking time further by salting the *soaking* water. Why? The sodium in the salt displaces the magnesium in the cellular walls. Sodium is soluble in ways that magnesium is not. The beans then cook faster.

But the water needs to be pretty salty. Try a teaspoon of salt for every cup of water. (Sometimes you can get by with a little less, depending on the bean varietal.) If you use two quarts of water, you might need eight teaspoons of salt. Once soaked, drain the beans in a colander in the sink and rinse them thoroughly to avoid an overly-salty soup.

One other thing: this intense magnesium/salt swap-out can put a drag on the bean's starches by keeping them tighter, less able to swell and turn tender as they cook. The inside of the beans can turn rather mealy.

That sort of compromise might not be worth shaving off the time. But it has nothing to do with adding a teaspoon of salt to a simmering pot of beans on the stove. Salt away, fellow bean lovers.

YOU MUST SOAK DRIED BEANS BEFORE COOKING THEM.

RULES ARE MEANT TO BE BROKEN.

You do not *have to* soak dried beans before you cook them. However, you might *want to* for culinary reasons.

Dried beans get tender by both water and heat.

☞ Water works its way slowly into the beans, rehydrating their collapsed cells and producing that starchy bite for which they're so highly prized.

☞ Heat works as it always does: realigning those cells, caramelizing essential sugars, and rendering everything more tasty and more tender. As Joan Crawford said in *The Women*: "If you throw a lamb chop in a hot oven, what's gonna keep it from gettin' done?"

Same with dried beans. If you throw them in a pot of broth and turn on the heat, nothing's gonna stop them from gettin' tender. However, heat works more quickly than water. So even when the beans are hot in the pot, the water has not yet penetrated all the way to their cores to render them soft and luscious.

By first soaking them in water, you're giving the water a head start. When the beans finally get in the pot, both the heat and water now work at about the same rate. In fact, by presoaking beans, you can reduce the cooking time, not by earth-shattering amounts, but by about 25 percent, sometimes less depending on the bean varietal.

Soak them for how long? About ten hours, changing the water once or twice. They'll swell pretty well within the first two hours but will need the rest of the time to fully hydrate.

You can speed this process up by first heating the beans to boiling in a big pot of water, boiling them for about 2 minutes, and then draining them in a colander set in the sink. Now put them in a big bowl, cover them with warm tap water, and soak for two hours.

So it's not that you *must* soak dried beans; it's that you *can*. Yes, cooking them unsoaked will take longer. And you run the risk of the heat working too quickly, making the beans mushy rather than toothsome. The secret is to keep the heat very low—low enough that you can count the bubbles as they form in the soup. And stir the pot occasionally, momentarily bringing down the broth's temperature to give the hydration process a leg up once in a while.

One benefit to not soaking the beans is that you'll end up with fewer moments of embarrassing gastric distress. Beans are full of complex sugars that we humans don't digest very well. If you cook beans for a long time, those sugars have a better chance of breaking down. Thus, the longer time on the stove will allow for greater sociability at the table, if you get our drift.

BLACK BEAN SOUP WITH LIME AND CILANTRO

8 bowlfuls

Bean soup doesn't have to be a two-day chore. It can be a comforting mélange of flavors and textures with little more effort than stirring. Oh, and a stocked pantry and spice rack. This dish goes well with a green salad topped by a vinegary dressing. (Note: Celeriac—a.k.a. celery root—is a pain to peel and dice. It is perhaps best to use both a knife and a vegetable peeler—the peeler for the smoother sections and the knife for the rifts and clefts. In any case, once peeled, you can slice it into ½-inch-thick rings, then dice these into little bits.)

2 tablespoons olive oil

1 medium yellow onion, chopped

1 medium green bell pepper, cored, seeded, and chopped

1 small celeriac, peeled and cut into ½-inch pieces

2 medium garlic cloves, minced

1 canned chipotle in adobo sauce, seeded and minced

3 tablespoons minced oregano leaves

1 tablespoon finely grated lime zest

1 tablespoon minced sage leaves

1 tablespoon ground cumin

½ teaspoon salt, or more as needed

½ teaspoon grated nutmeg

8 cups canned, reduced-sodium, fat-free chicken broth

2 cups (or 1 pound) dried black beans, picked
   over for any broken shells and then rinsed

¼ cup minced cilantro leaves

2 tablespoons lime juice

1. Heat a big pot over medium heat, then swirl in the oil. Dump in the onion, bell pepper, and celeriac.

2. Add the garlic and minced chipotle (1 *canned* chipotle, not 1 can of chipotles). Give them a few quick stirs, then stir in the oregano, lime zest, sage, cumin, ½ teaspoon salt, and the nutmeg. You don't have to grate your own; you can use ground nutmeg, but use only ¼ teaspoon because it's more pungent, less subtle, mostly because of long storage.

3. Pour in the broth and stir well to get any browned bits up off the pot's bottom and sides. Then stir in the beans. Raise the heat to medium-high and bring the whole thing to a full simmer, even a low boil, stirring once in a while.

4. Cover the pot, reduce the heat to low, and simmer slowly until the beans are tender, about 3 hours. Yep, 3. There's no rushing this thing. You want a very low simmer, just a few bubbles at a time. And you want to stir it every once in a while. But there's not much else to worry about. Go do whatever it is you do while a big pot of bean soup cooks on the stove. And by the way, there's only one way to know if it's done: taste a bean. It should be tender with a slight amount of give just at its core, just a little toothsomeness.

5. Just before serving, stir in the cilantro and lime juice. These will brighten the flavors from their duller, earthy mellowness. Then taste again to see if it needs a little more salt. Try the soup with a dollop of sour cream or yogurt on each serving. Or some pita chips on the side for a little crunch.

REFRIED BEANS ARE FRIED TWICE.

THIS TRAIN OF THOUGHT HAS NO CABOOSE.

You may associate refried beans with that awful wallpaper paste that passes itself off as a side dish in some Mexican restaurants. Which is a tragedy. Because bona fide refried beans are a thing of beauty.

No, they're not fried twice. Only once.

This myth stems from a mistranslation. The Spanish name for this silky side dish is *frijoles refritos* (*free-HO-lays ray-FREE-tohs*). That little *re-* is the culprit. Yes, it can mean *again,* as it does in English, as in *reunite* or *redo.* But particularly in some Mexican dialects, *re-* can be an intensifier. *Retebien* means *very, very good,* not just *tebien,* or *very good.*

So *refritos* actually means *well-fried.* Or *fried in the best way imaginable.* Probably because there's lard involved.

Here's how it all works. Refried beans start with dried beans. And usually *not* presoaked dried beans. These are tossed into a pot of water or stock, most often with some lard added for good measure, and then cooked—and cooked and cooked until they're mush.

Then they're smashed against the sides of the pot with the back of a wooden spoon until they're a grainy paste.

Or they're smushed with a potato masher until smooth. Or they're put through a food mill so that there are no bean skins left at all.

When everyone's at the table, a big skillet is heated over medium-high heat. Once it's *rehot,* a fat is added—again, most often, lard. Chopped onions now go in as well—and occasionally, diced and seeded green bell peppers. These are stirred until soft, then in goes the bean paste for a hot sizzle in the creamy fat and vegetables. Sounds ridiculously good, right?

Unfortunately, way too many Mexican restaurants cut corners. They don't add onions, certainly not bell peppers. And the beans themselves are not fried a second time. Instead, the mushy purée is merely warmed for hours in trays back in the kitchen.

But if you ever find yourself in a genuine Mexican restaurant where the refried beans are made to order, jump at the chance. It will be a revelation. And the lard will make your hair real shiny the next day.

SQUEEZE A PEACH TO TELL IF IT'S RIPE.

STOP IT RIGHT NOW.

Please don't manhandle the peaches. It's not polite to squeeze them, then toss them away. It makes them feel cheap.

But without squeezing one, you might ask, *how will I know the thing's ripe?*

Herein lies the problem with all drupes—a.k.a. stone fruits. That is, plums, apricots, pluots, even cherries, and yes, peaches. How do you know when you've got a good one?

Use these three tests:

 1. Avoid the green.

As a stone fruit ripens, the chlorophyll layer disappears and the brighter colors show through. Go for gorgeously golden peaches with a pink tinge—or blood red cherries, not the pale ones. But color is still not a perfect guide to ripeness. Sometimes, a perfectly yellow apricot is tasteless. Which is why you should . . .

2. Pick it up.

A ripe stone fruit should feel heavy. It matures on the tree by developing more and more water-soluble pectin and complex sugars, replacing starches, acids, and protective chemical defenses. The fruit gets soft, sure—but more important, it gets bloated and thus hefty as it holds more and more moisture in its cells. Squeezing it won't tell you this tale. Heaviness is not softness. A soft drupe can well be a mealy drupe. Which is why you should . . .

3. Smell it.

This one's the key. If it doesn't smell like anything, it won't taste like anything. Put a piece of fruit to your nose. Breathe in, particularly the stem end. Does the peach (or nectarine or apricot or what have you) have an irresistible aroma? Then go ahead and bite down. (Well, buy it first. And wash it, too. Because God knows how many other people have picked it up and squeezed it.)

Let's face it: ripening is the final phase of life. The fruit is getting ready to die. And die it must in order for its seeds to get broadcast into the world for the next generation. So it's gotten all tarted up for its last chance to be loved, like Yvonne DeCarlo in Sondheim's *Follies*. Or Lindsay Lohan in just about anything.

Soon, the drupe's flesh will give way to rot, liquefying as the starches break down so that the pit has a little bit of pure sugar to send it on its way into the big, bad world.

Not a whit of that process is enhanced by squeezing. In fact, doing so bruises the fruit—and starts that whole polyphenol oxidase reaction happening, the one that caused the browning trouble with the avocados and guacamole.

So be gentle with the peaches. They're juicy wonders, here today, gone tomorrow.

TAP A WATERMELON TO TELL IF IT'S SWEET.

BEEN THERE, DONE THAT, DON'T NEED TO AGAIN.

Apparently picking a good watermelon remains a mystery for a lot of people. That must be why they resort to mamboing with it at the supermarket. They stand in the produce section, shaking that watermelon for all its worth. While we're for public dancing, it really doesn't do much for a watermelon—though if you hear sloshing water inside, you've got way more problems than the stares of your fellow shoppers. The thing's about to liquefy.

Then there are the tappers. Like safe crackers, these people thump and flick the poor watermelon, searching for a certain sound. Too bad not a one of them can describe the sound they want to hear. We once asked an alleged expert, a prominent vegetarian cookbook author, to explain the required resonance.

"Somewhere between a thud and a ping," she said.

What's *between* a thud and a ping? A *thing*? A *pud*? You want your watermelon to sound like a *pud*? Even if you can explain what the heck a *thing* or a *pud* is, you still won't know how sweet the watermelon is.

Which is the point of this whole exercise.

Let's get one thing straight: a watermelon isn't a fruit. So that smell test we developed for peaches, apricots, and stone fruits won't work.

A watermelon is a vegetable, related to cucumbers. The most reliable test for its sweetness has to do with a pea vinelike tendril that comes off the stem next to the vine that attached the behemoth to its plant. That pigtail tendril should be brown, dry, and curly without being desiccated or friable.

Although you can find watermelons with their tendrils intact at fruit stands, most at the supermarket are missing them. In which case, you should first check the color. A ripe watermelon should have a faint bleaching or fading between the strips in the skin.

Of course, not all watermelons have stripes. Some are round, dark green balls. So there's a second test: turn the watermelon over, exposing its underbelly where it rested on the ground. That spot should be creamy white or pale yellow. There should be no green under there, nor any sign of stripes. If so, the watermelon is underripe, picked too soon. And if that spot is brown, the watermelon is overripe, maybe even fermenting inside.

Seedless watermelons are a particularly difficult crop. They must be pollinated by a seeded varietal. However, the two varietals cannot be planted right next to each other: seedless sugar babies cannot be grown next to seeded sugar babies, not because anything will happen to either, but because the farmer won't know which is which in the field. Also, there are still seeds in the seedless watermelons. But they're actually faux seeds, caused by stress in the plant—often because of weather, but also by soil conditions and overfertilization. Best then to look for farmers at our local green markets who take care and caution over their melons.

Now you know. And now you can go find a better mambo partner than a watermelon.

WATERMELON GAZPACHO

About 10 cups, or 6 servings

Gazpacho is a chilled, summer soup, a favorite around the Mediterranean. This is a thoroughly American version, the watermelon bits replacing the tomatoes for a sweet, light, refreshing twist, best as a first course and it goes wonderfully with anything off the grill or even a good old-fashioned grilled cheese sandwich. Because watermelons are sweeter than tomatoes, we've upped the vegetables quite a bit to make sure that there's a good balance of ingredients. And since you know how to pick a perfect watermelon, you can have perfect summer bliss every time.

1 large, ripe, seedless, red watermelon
2 cucumbers
1 medium yellow bell pepper, cored, seeded, and minced

1 medium orange bell pepper, cored, seeded, and minced
1 medium shallot, minced
2 tablespoons lemon juice
2 tablespoons white wine vinegar
1 teaspoon salt
Several dashes hot red pepper sauce,
  such as Tabasco sauce

1. First, you need to deal with the watermelon. Split the watermelon in half lengthwise, then use a melon baller or a spoon to begin digging out balls and mounds of the flesh. Flick away any seeds. Once you've got about 8 cups of watermelon flesh, put it in a food processor fitted with a chopping blade or in a large blender. Pulse or blend just until puréed, scraping down the inside of the canister to make sure everything gets whirred up.

2. Peel the cucumbers, then halve them lengthwise. Run a spoon down the inside of the cut sides, scooping out and discarding the seeds and their water pockets. Mince the flesh into tiny bits. Put these in a serving bowl, then pour in the watermelon purée.

3. Stir in everything else: the bell peppers (if you can't find an orange bell pepper, two yellow ones will do), shallot, lemon juice, vinegar, salt, and hot red pepper sauce. Stir, then cover the bowl and refrigerate the soup for at least 4 hours or overnight. It can last in the refrigerator for up to 3 days—but it's so tasty, it won't.

MYTH #58

CHEWING CELERY NEGATES
ITS CALORIES.

IF IGNORANCE IS BLISS, WHY
AREN'T MORE PEOPLE HAPPY?

Somewhere, somehow, there must be a food out there that contains fewer calories than it takes to eat it. Anyone who's ever had a few pounds to shed has had that thought at one time or another.

First off, chewing doesn't use up many calories. On average, about five per hour. If you're going hell-bent-for-leather on a piece of gum, maybe eleven per hour.

More so than chewing, digesting food burns calories. And here, there may be something that almost validates the celery myth. And the chile myth. And the cabbage myth. And the garlic myth. And the turnip myth. And the cucumber myth. And the carrot myth.

All these—and more, like broccoli and beet greens—have been identified as calorie-negative foods. These are ostensibly so low in calories that you burn more energy digesting them than they hold in the first place.

Not exactly. Celery has about six calories per stalk. So one stalk may indeed have negative calories—provided you chew it for a very long time. Not the full hour, but perhaps twenty minutes or so. One stalk of celery, twenty minutes of chomping. Oh, well, there's two calories down. And digesting it will then burn about five more. So you're one calorie ahead of the game (with a sore jaw to boot).

But don't break out one-calorie worth of champagne just yet. The minute you add a second stalk of celery, you just bumped yourself up and over the chew/digestion calorie intake limit. It doesn't take appreciably more calories to digest two stalks than it did to digest just one. So you'd better chew longer. Say, a good ninety minutes on those two celery stalks.

Yes, you may lose weight if you chew on celery rather than reaching for a slice of lemon poppy seed cheesecake or a bag of barbecue-flavored potato chips. But you're losing weight because you're substituting a healthy vegetable for a decadent if delicious treat.

And yes, if you eat nothing but celery and chew it like mad, *nonstop, all day*, you will lose weight—because you'll end up with a slight calorie imbalance, fewer in than out. But don't get too excited. It's an imbalance of at most twenty calories over the course of the day. Since you need to burn three thousand calories to shed one pound of fat, it's not as if that imbalance is going to get you in a Speedo or a bikini by summertime.

It may, however, make you spend more time in the bathroom because those celery stalks are full of fiber. Which is also a way to lose weight. Although not entirely a pleasant or smart way.

APRICOT PITS CONTAIN CYANIDE.

A LITTLE KNOWLEDGE IS A DANGEROUS THING.

All the pits of the fruiting members of the rose family—apricots, cherries, peaches, apples, and crabapples—contain amygdaline. It's also known as vitamin B_{17}, or laetrile, the touted miracle cancer cure from the '70s. Because of a digestive reaction deep down inside you, sugary amygdaline breaks down into—ta da!—hydrogen cyanide gas.

So apricot pits don't *contain* cyanide. They contain a cyanogenic compound.

But apricots aren't the only homicidal food. Amygdaline and other cyanogenic compounds are found in more than two thousand edible species of plants, including cassava, corn, sorghum, millet, all sorts of broad beans, and many nuts.

Ingest enough amygdaline and you'll be pushing up daisies. But enough is quite a lot. Because hydrogen cyanide gas passes through and out of you rather quickly. Your body is rather keen to get rid of it, as you can imagine.

What's more, the minute you heat a fruit or a veggie rich in amygdaline, you destroy its ability to kill you. The amygdaline breaks down. Which is why you don't hear about too many people trying to off themselves with cooked fava beans.

All that said, even your body's natural desire to overcome a poisonous gas can be overwhelmed. The highest amount of amygdaline is found in bitter almonds, a particularly pernicious version of those tasty nuts we used to tart up with barbecue spices, cinnamon sugar mixes, and other indignities during the hey-ho '60s. But it takes between fifty and seventy bitter almonds to do you in. And because the gas disperses, you have to eat them quite quickly, in just a few minutes. In fact, your own metabolism may thwart your plans, depending on how quickly or slowly the nuts exit your digestive tract.

By contrast, apricot pits have far less amygdaline. So you'd need to eat more than a hundred of those little buggers in about a minute to have a chance at doing yourself in. Even Joey Chestnut would have a hard time pulling that one off.

SPINACH IS HIGH IN IRON.

YES, BUT ACTUALLY NO.

For years, we tortured children with this myth. We forced them to sit at the table, staring down a dark green pile of mushy leaves. *It's good for you,* we said.

It's the fault of yet another German. (So much of the last two centuries was.) In 1870, Professor E. von Wolff put a decimal point in the wrong place and came to the astounding conclusion that spinach had almost as much iron as red meat.

Nobody caught the error. Probably because along came Weimar Germany. And wild Berlin nightclubs. People weren't too interested in fixing decimal points, what with the rampant sexual experimentation of the time.

Then came Popeye. There's no evidence that spinach was made his steroid of choice because of the professor's faulty calculations. But it was sure lucky. That sailor's fascination with the leafy green led to the salvation of collapsing spinach prices in the United States. Combine industry and myth, add a cartoon character, and you've got sales. If in doubt, open any food magazine published in the last hundred years and check out the ads.

In truth, spinach has about as much iron as any other leafy green. And the iron in spinach consists of mostly just one of the two types found in our dietary choices. The *non-heme* variety in spinach (that is, not found in blood but rather in plants) is not absorbed well by us. By contrast, the *heme* variety, mostly found in meat, is absorbed very well.

Spinach also has lots of oxalic acid. Which happens to be an iron-absorption inhibitor. Thus, when you eat spinach, you absorb less iron than it has to offer. What's more, oxalic acid loves to bind with calcium. When it does so, it becomes an even bigger iron-absorption inhibitor. So if you eat your spinach with a little grated cheese, you'll take in even less iron.

If you're so concerned about getting all your iron from vegetables, eat collards, turnip greens, or broccoli. These are relatively low in that inhibiting oxalic acid but high in iron (although it is of the *non-heme* variety).

And while you're at it, have some spinach, too. Just don't boil it down into a mushy paste. Instead, have it stir-fried with garlic and rice vinegar. And grill up a steak to go alongside. Because that's where you'll get most of your iron.

A PINCH OF SUGAR PRESERVES THE COLOR OF COOKED VEGETABLES.

CAN'T BE, NEVER WAS.

Indeed, sugar can make vegetables taste a little better, particularly those that are not at their prime. Thus, people add sugar to a pot of simmering tomato sauce, particularly if the tomatoes were mushy, unripe, or bruised.

We're omnivores. We value a range of flavors to find satiety. So a sweet backdrop foregrounds other tastes—like the sour and even slightly bitter notes in that marinara. Ta da! A bigger range of flavors and more satisfaction in each bite.

In the same manner, a little salt in a lemon pie makes it taste both sweeter and more sour. And a little sugar in a broccoli purée suppresses a few of the bitter notes, creating a more mellow, middle-of-the-road flavor.

But it all has nothing to do with preserving color. Green vegetables change color when they cook because the heat brings the chlorophyll to the surface, turning them momentarily more green. Steam some sugar snap peas for a few minutes, or cook them in a little olive oil in a skillet over medium heat for no more than a minute. They turn a lovely neon green. However, if you continue to cook them, the chlorophyll will begin to fall apart. They soon turn a dull olive green—and with enough time, a puky yellow.

Acid has the same effect—which is why lettuce can turn sickly yellow if it sits around in a vinaigrette overnight. Which is also why you should dress a green salad only at the last minute to avoid dull, squishy leaves. To exacerbate matters, as vegetables cook, they release their own natural acids, which do what vinegar does: they aid in the breakdown of chlorophyll.

Sugar won't stop this breakdown. It might make the attending vegetables taste a little better, but it's not going to preserve color.

And really, a pinch of sugar isn't that effective a seasoning. Think about it: a pinch in a big pot? Sure, there might be some minimal change. But for real results, you'd need more than that. And how much sugar do you want to eat? Just go for better, riper vegetables; roast, steam, or stir-fry them just until they're crisp-tender; and skip the doctoring.

A ROAD MAP FOR ROAST VEGETABLES

Figure on about ¾ pound of raw vegetables per person

This is a road map, rather than a recipe. It'll tell you how to roast vegetables until they're caramelized and sweet, no sugar necessary. But you'll have to figure things out as you go along. Just remember this: we are most sated with a range of textures and tastes. So choose vegetables from several categories and mix them together. (Note: Purple beets stain everything purple, which is not the worst thing, but it's good to know for presentation purposes.)

1. Position the rack in the center of the oven and preheat the oven to 375°F.

2. Now choose the vegetables. We've got four groups, each with its own timing.

Those that take 1$\frac{1}{2}$ hours:

Potatoes, particularly yellow-fleshed or red-skinned, cubed

Beets, peeled and cubed

Rutabaga (sometimes called yellow or wax turnips), peeled and cubed

Parsnips, peeled and cut into $\frac{1}{2}$-inch-thick rings

Carrots, peeled and cut into $\frac{1}{2}$-inch-thick rings

Those that take 1 hour:

Butternut squash, peeled, halved, seeded, and cubed

Buttercup squash, peeled, halved, seeded, and cubed

Acorn squash, peeled, halved, seeded, and cubed

Delicata squash, halved, seeded, and cubed

Those that take 45 minutes:

Onions, peeled and quartered

Shallots, peeled

Garlic cloves, peeled

Those that take 30 minutes:

Broccoli florets and thinly sliced stems

Cauliflower florets

Brussels sprouts, larger ones halved

Asparagus spears, peeled

3. Weigh the total amount of vegetables you've chosen. You'll need 2 tablespoons olive oil, ½ teaspoon salt (preferably kosher salt), and ½ teaspoon freshly ground black pepper *for every pound*.

4. Now roast them. Start by tossing the longest cooking ones you've chosen in a big roasting pan or on a lipped baking sheet with the olive oil, salt, and pepper. Remember that they need a lot of room—and you'll be adding more. Put the pan or baking sheet in the oven and set your timer. Then add other types of vegetable at the appropriate time.

For example, if you're roasting potatoes, carrots, Brussels sprouts, and shallots, start with the potatoes and carrots for 45 minutes, then add the shallots, roast those with the roots for 15 more minutes, then add the Brussels sprouts.

Stir the vegetables occasionally as they roast, usually every 15 minutes or so.

5. Right at the end of roasting, if you desire, you can toss in a little balsamic vinegar, just to brighten the flavors—just a splash, no more than a tablespoon or so. Stir it up and you're done.

7

SOME DAY YOUR PRINCE WILL COME

Myths You May Have Heard from Your Bubbe, Abuela, MeeMaw, or Some Other Random Old Person

Just because an old person says something, it doesn't mean it's true. We realize that we've just invalidated half the campaign strategies for the U.S. Senate, but the medium does not validate the message.

Of course, myths thrive on repetition. But they also need external validation. Enter an old person, someone who has supposedly gleaned wisdom from time.

These days, wisdom is too often confused with crankiness. We've reached a point where incivility and irritability pass themselves off as truth-telling. But think about it: would you take modern dating advice from your grandmother? Especially after she's lived so many years with your grandfather?

These eleven myths are some of the moldy oldies, the sage advice of bygone generations, still hanging around cookbooks, blog postings, and ill-researched magazine articles. It's time they were put to rest.

Bottom line, don't trust anyone over thirty. Or under thirty, for that matter. Verify. You'll be much less cranky.

MYTH #62

EATING CANDY CAUSES ACNE.

MOUTHS WORK BETTER WHEN THEY'RE CONNECTED TO BRAINS.

Just because something tastes good doesn't mean it will do you in. Desire and damnation are not automatically bound together, no matter how many cranky old people want to make it so.

In fact, juried medical studies have shown *no* link between the consumption of candy and an outbreak of acne. Most of the time, acne is caused by three factors:

1. Overactive oil glands.

These are stimulated by the production of androgens, the major male hormones, but produced by both genders. Teenagers produce more hormones than adults, so they also produce more androgen. Teenage boys produce more androgen than girls, so the onslaught of acne is usually worse in boys. But androgen itself is not a bad thing. It stimulates and regulates the growth spurts during puberty. It is now thought to regulate the function of many internal organs, including the kidney, liver, and (of course) the reproductive tract. With more androgen, boys' voices deepen and they sprout facial hair. And those oil glands begin slowly turning that baby face into a sexy twentysomething—although sometimes those glands go into hyperdrive and start clogging up. See a good case of acne around your house? You may be looking at the next Justin Bieber.

 ### 2. Stress.

Androgens are the basic component of our fight-or-flight response. As we said, boys are awash in them. Add stress and you get a more pronounced fight-or-flight response and thus more androgens, particularly during adolescence. For boys, there may be little help except topical remedies—although less stress can't hurt. Stop pushing him to join a third after-school club and his face might take a turn for the better. Teenage girls, too, could do with less stress—although estrogen is itself a great defense against acne. Put your daughter on the pill and her face may clear up. Of course, you might have a few other problems to contend with.

 ### 3. Blocked pores.

Our natural defense against attacks on the skin is a routine, good-guy bacteria called *propionibarterium acnes*. These are tough fighters, keeping bad bacteria at bay. However, they also can get walled into oil-filled pores—and go a little haywire, multiplying out of control. Voilà, le zit.

To get rid of acne, use a topical solution like benzoyl peroxide or salicylic acid as directed by the label. A nonalcoholic toner can also help. Beyond those, certain run-of-the-mill antibiotics like amoxicillin work. And beyond even those, you can call out the big-gun drugs like isotretinoin, which really dry things up.

But taking the candy away won't do a thing to improve anybody's complexion.

GUM STAYS IN YOUR STOMACH FOR 7, 10, 13 ... A MILLION YEARS.

AND WE'VE GOT A BRIDGE FOR SALE, TOO.

Every now and again, you may find yourself in the predicament of having nowhere to dispose of your gum gracefully. Go ahead and swallow with dignity. Your body will do what it always does: it will digest what it can and dispose of the rest.

In case you missed it in biology class, here's how it works: you drop something edible down your gullet. It sticks around your stomach—with its very caustic acids—for a limited amount of time, just a few minutes in the case of most sugars, several hours in the case of the various fibers from whole grains. Your stomach then flushes everything out into your intestines, where it's pushed constantly down toward, well, you know where.

That goes for the digestible and the indigestible bits. Yes, some pieces of chewing gum fall in the latter camp. Those are the parts pushed on down the track intact toward their inevitable conclusion. Along with a whole lot of other indigestibles, including every single gram of insoluble fiber you ever swallow.

And yes, too many indigestible bits can cause problems. If you swallowed too many sticks of gum—like five hundred or so, one every three minutes day and night for twenty-four hours straight—then you might end up with those indigestible bits all bound together, forming a bezoar (*BEE-zoar*), a rocky aggregate of indigestible materials, common in ruminants but possible in all mammals.

It will need to be expunged in the hospital. But you won't have to wait three or five or however many years to find out if you've got said bezoar. You'll be hunched over in a matter of hours. Which, frankly, is a fate you deserve if you swallowed five hundred sticks of gum.

In a healthy person, the colon lining continually regenerates, renewed by resident stem cells. The lining remains whole while the cellular composition changes almost constantly. You're always shedding bits of it. If something were to sit down there for years, it would have to survive this incessant turnover. Which it can't. And if it did, it would rot. Your intestines would fester, then rupture. Back to the hospital with you. If not the morgue.

But the occasional piece of gum is really not going to gum up the works.

THE FIVE SECOND RULE: IF FOOD FALLS ON THE FLOOR, YOU'VE GOT FIVE SECONDS TO PICK IT UP.

SORRY, BUT NO.

This one stems from a partial truth: the longer a piece of food stays in contact with a contaminated surface, the more microbes it will pick up. But *more* is a relative term. In five seconds, it has already picked up a lot. So while it can pick up even more germs in another five seconds, the damage has already been done.

Research carried out by Paul Dawson at Clemson University has shown that a bologna sandwich left on a salmonella-contaminated tile floor for five seconds will have picked up as many as eight thousand microbes. Too bad it only takes ten microbes to deliver the infectious dose. For deadly strains of E. coli, the get-sick number is about a hundred. That's a really small count when we're talking about microscopic organisms, but it's perfectly doable in five seconds.

Bacteria are adherent. They glom onto things, including your digestive track, like Facebook stalkers.

But you probably don't wash your floors with salmonella. While researchers were smearing theirs with bad gunk, you may have been cleaning yours with an antibacterial wash. It's true: clean floors in well-kept residential homes have, on average, few bad pests per square inch.

But don't kid yourself: few is not none. Any number of germs infest our floors, mostly because of the stuff we track inside. And we're talking about tile here. Let's not even mention carpet. If you want to cut down on the amount of microscopic gunk on your floors, take your shoes off and leave them outside.

Even so, when it comes to food dropped on the floor, it's a roll of the dice. And not just any dice. Dice that are stacked against you. So the next time you drop something on the floor, something that you're actually going to put in your mouth, first consider *which floor* it's been on. And then ask yourself if you really need to eat something you scraped off the floor. If the answer is yes, you should probably take a good, hard look at your life.

DRIED SPICES LAST INDEFINITELY.

NO DICE.

Dried herbs and spices age like all of us—except faster. Eventually, they take on the flavor profile of dust. A teaspoon of the stuff in your vacuum cleaner bag will have about the same effect in a pot of soup as the stuff in that five-year-old bottle of dried oregano.

How long will these dried bits of flavor last on your pantry shelf? Depends on what they are.

An herb is the leafy bits of an aromatic, seed-producing, annual plant: basil, thyme, or oregano. Almost all herbs are green. They are sold fresh in the produce section or dried in the spice aisle.

By contrast, a spice is a dried fruit, berry, flower, root, seed, husk, or bark of a woody or herbaceous plant. A spice is typically used in smaller amounts than an herb: paprika (fruit), ginger (root), cinnamon (bark), peppercorns (berries), or mace (husk). They are mostly sold dried in the spice aisle— with some exceptions (like fresh ginger).

To confuse the matter, some plants give us both herbs and spices. Cilantro leaves are an herb; the plant's seeds, a spice (a.k.a. coriander). And some spices, particularly in Asian cultures, can be made from non-plant life forms. Ground dried seahorse, anyone?

If stored properly . . .

Fresh herbs will last about one week, if stored as you would lettuce;

Fresh spices, maybe two weeks, if stored in the fridge;

Dried herbs, one year, maybe two;

Ground spices, at most three years;

Whole dried spices, maybe three to four years;

Most extracts, about four years;

And vanilla extract, at least five years.

How do you know if the dried bottlings you've got are still good? Follow these guidelines:

1. If the color of a dried herb looks ashy, the taste will be, too.

2. No herb or spice should have a tea-like tang—or smell like dust. Take a little from the bottle and crush it in your palm. Does it smell as it's supposed to?

3. Store dried herbs and spices in a cool, dark place, away from the stove and dishwasher—and away from the light.

4. Moisture will destroy dried herbs over time. Never stick a wet measuring spoon in the bottle. And never pour an herb or a spice straight from a bottle into a steaming pot of soup.

In the end, follow the same advice for dried herbs and spices that you would for dating: if in doubt, swap it out.

COCONUT FISH CURRY

Serves 4, goes well with white rice

Here's an elegant way to cook thicker fish fillets: cod, halibut, and the like—or even snapper fillets, provided they're at least 1 inch thick. With slow oven-poaching, the fish stays moist, nestled into an aromatic curry that becomes the sauce, ladled into individual bowls of rice. The dried spices have to be fresh—a dinner like this deserves the best!

One 2-inch-piece lemongrass, white and pale green parts
    only, thinly sliced into little rings
Up to 1 whole serrano or Thai hot
    chile, halved and seeded
1 medium garlic clove, quartered
2 whole cloves
1 tablespoon cumin seeds
1 teaspoon ground coriander
1 teaspoon ground cinnamon
1 teaspoon turmeric

1½ *pounds skinless thick-fleshed white fish fillets, such*
   as cod, bass, or halibut, cut into 4 equal pieces
About 1 cup dry white wine or dry vermouth
2 medium scallions, minced
1½ *tablespoons fresh ginger, peeled and minced*
6 ounces thinly sliced shiitake mushroom caps
¼ *cup coconut milk, regular or reduced fat*
2 teaspoons soy sauce, regular or reduced sodium
Minced basil leaves, for garnish

1. Place the lemongrass, chile, garlic, cloves, cumin seeds, coriander, cinnamon, and turmeric in a small spice grinder, a mini food processor, or a mortar. Grind the spices or mash them with a pestle until they make a coarse curry paste. Make sure you repeatedly scrape down the insides of the canister or the mortar so that everything is getting crushed into the pulpy, grainy mass. Set aside.

2. Position the rack in the center of the oven and preheat the oven to 400°F. Lay the fish fillets in a lidded, 12-inch, oven-safe sauté pan or a large, lidded, high-sided skillet. Pour in enough wine to come halfway up the fillets in the pan.

3. Without ever heating them, transfer the fillets from the pan or skillet to a cutting board. Measure them to see how thick they are at the thickest point. Why? You'll see.

4. Add the scallions, ginger, and up to 1 tablespoon of the prepared curry paste to the wine in the pan. Bring to a simmer over medium-high heat. Yes, you've made more curry paste than you need. Save it in the fridge, covered, for about two weeks to be used as a rub for fish or shrimp on the grill, to provide the aromatic spices in a stir-fry, or just to have another go at this dish.

5. Stir in the mushrooms; cover tightly, reduce the heat to low, and simmer until the mushrooms have started to get tender, about 4 minutes. Partially submerge the fish fillets in the sauce, bring everything back to a simmer, then cover and place in the oven for about 7 minutes for each inch of thickness. (See page 215.)

6. Transfer the cooked fish to individual serving bowls. Set the pan back over medium-high heat, bring the liquid to a low simmer, and stir in the coconut milk and soy sauce. Divide the sauce and vegetables among the bowls. Garnish with the minced basil leaves.

SALADS AND SPREADS MADE WITH MAYONNAISE SPOIL QUICKLY.

COULD BE, BUT MAYBE NOT.

There are two factors in spoilage when it comes to mayo.

☞ First, temperature. Keep those salads and spreads below 40°F or above 140°F for safety's sake.

☞ And second, acid. It wards off many food-borne pests.

With a ph around 4.0, commercial mayonnaise is pretty acidic, comparable to coffee and beer. It's not a good nursery for bacteria. Yes, unrefrigerated, wet coffee grounds will eventually mold. But it takes a while. Similarly, the mayonnaise is probably not the culprit in that bowl of salad festering in the heat on the picnic table.

The ham is. Or the chicken. Or the tuna. And the potatoes. And the hard-boiled eggs. And all the vegetables. Even the onions. Those things will spoil despite the acidity of the mayonnaise, mostly because it doesn't penetrate all the way down into them but instead stays smeared along their surface planes. Unlike bad bacteria.

Yes, given enough time and a prolonged, warm (not hot) temperature, even mayonnaise will spoil. Its acidity will break down and the fun-killing pests will chow down on the attendant sugars and fats.

That said, we've been discussing commercial mayonnaise. When it comes to homemade mayo, the ph is higher—and so its acidic profile is lower. Plus, homemade mayonnaise is usually made with raw eggs. Out of their shells, those don't fare too well unrefrigerated.

So if you think that salad at your next picnic was made with homemade mayonnaise, stay your distance. Or do the math: divide the number of bathrooms by the number of guests. But fear not the jarred mayonnaise in that salad, just mind the temperature.

And one more thing: an ice cooler isn't a great place for your salad—unless you fill said cooler clear to the brim with ice and keep refilling it with new ice as the old melts. A thin layer of ice on the bottom of a shoddy cooler isn't going to do much for your health beyond keeping the sweat off the food.

BUTTER SPOILS QUICKLY IF IT'S NOT REFRIGERATED.

EVENTUALLY, REALLY EVENTUALLY.

Butter goes rancid because of four factors, in this order of importance:

☞ **Air.** Or more precisely, the oxygen in the air. In short order, butter fats can oxygenate and turn rancid. Plus, the residual milk solids are going to get none too savory, as if you left milk out on the counter for days.

☞ **Light.** It also degrades those luscious fatty acids, snapping them apart so the dangling acid chains recombine into foul-tasting bits.

☞ **Natural enzymes and microbes.** These love the taste of sweet, creamy butter, too!

☞ **Heat.** This one's an ancillary factor, of less importance, more of a way to speed up the first two factors. We're talking a consistent temperature a little higher than you'd keep your home, somewhere above 80°F, depending on the many internal factors in the milk that

was used to produce the butter. Since heat speeds up
the reaction, most people put butter in the fridge to put
the brakes on the whole process. But cold, hard butter
and warm toast do not make a happy couple.

Unfortunately, some people get all up in arms over the
problem of the heat. They advise storing butter in the freezer
only, a sort of deep chill to solve all wrongs. But butter out of
the freezer is even more maddening to spread than the stuff
out of the fridge.

What's more, butter can go rancid in the fridge, after eight
weeks or so, as well as in the freezer after several months.

So what's the best butter-storage solution for people who
like to spread it on toast? A butter bell. It seals butter into
a small container that is then turned upside down in a jar
of cool water. The butter is safeguarded against oxygen and
light. If you change the water every few days, it's safeguarded
against heat, too, except on the most beastly days. The butter
bell will then keep the butter at room temperature for several
weeks, a boon to all us spreaders.

OILING THE WATER KEEPS THE PASTA FROM STICKING.

ONLY ON DAYS THAT DON'T END IN "Y."

Pasta is made from wheat. The best sorts are made from durum wheat, a particularly hard varietal. But even durum gets sticky, doing what wheat does when it gets hot and moist.

If you add oil to the bubbling water in the pot, the pasta may not stick together. But it's not because of the oil. Most of it will wash down the drain in the colander. The little bit that remains will simply cause the sauce to slide off the noodles. Which is a tragedy. Most of the time, pasta *should* stick. That way, it holds the sauce.

The only good way to keep pasta from sticking in the pot is to stir it a few times after it hits the boiling water. When the noodles first go for a swim, the surface starches absorb water like sponges and blow up. Eventually, they pop, releasing their starch into the water. The key moment lies between the two, between the absorbing and the popping. If you stir the pot a few times during the first two or three minutes of cooking, you'll keep the pasta from glomming together, as those sticky granules begin to grow in bulk.

You also need a large pot with quite a bit of water, about four quarts for every pound of pasta. If you don't, the starch will not disperse evenly and can lead to stickiness on the noodles again.

How do you know when pasta is done? Sure, there are cooking times listed on packages, offering guidelines (not rules). The only way to be sure is to pull a piece out of the water and taste it. It should be *al dente*—in other words, there should be a slight amount of resistance (or a slight amount of *tooth,* in culinary terms) in each piece of pasta.

Some people say you should oil the pasta water, not to keep the pasta from sticking, but so that the water itself doesn't boil over in the pot. Yes, that bit's true. Here's why. Water molecules are polar, so they line up to create pretty good surface tension. The pasta in the pot releases its starch and other impurities, which break the surface tension of those water molecules. The resulting mix rises up as foam, which can overflow the pot. A little added oil will restabilize the tension. It disperses into zillions of tiny droplets that pop the bubbles of any forming foam.

But a better solution is to use a bigger pot and more water so as not to lose the right pasta texture that will hold the sauce. The bigger the pot, the more water you can use, and so the more diluted the impurities—so the less effect they have on the surface tension and the less chance there is that the pot will overflow.

RINSE THE COOKED PASTA BEFORE USING IT.

COULD BE BUT NOT ALWAYS.

Or is it *don't rinse the cooked pasta before using it*? There are actually two sets of adherents: the rinsers (mostly home cooks who find their pasta too sticky) and the non-rinsers (mostly professional chefs and almost all Italians). Like a good mom mediating between siblings, we can honestly say, "You're both right."

It all goes back to the sticky pasta debate. That stickiness is natural Velcro. When you toss freshly cooked pasta into a sauce in a skillet, the starches on the outside of the pasta pick up the sauce and hold it to the noodles. They also peel off more starches to further thicken the sauce—two benefits in one!

However, if you don't have impeccable timing and cook the pasta before the sauce is done, you might want to rinse the pasta. Otherwise, you'll end up with the noodles stuck into one big clump in the colander.

Hot pasta right out of its cooking water will indeed hold the sauce better. But the longer the noodles sit around in the colander, the more their starches glom onto one another, eventually morphing into a tangled mess that won't hold much of anything. Even worse, cooked, cool, but *unrinsed* pasta can turn into a sticky nightmare and ruin a pasta salad. And that's not to mention the hassle of building a lasagna with unrinsed sheets of cooked pasta that stick together and tear into shreds. It's not worth the effort.

In the end, here are the facts:

☞ 1. Don't rinse the pasta if you're tossing it into a bubbling sauce in a skillet or saucepan.

It will hold that sauce and make it more luscious. But be sure to get the sauce ready before the pasta is done and keep it warm on the back burner of the stove. That way, you can quickly bring it back up to a nice simmer and toss it with the still-hot unrinsed pasta, which will now pick up that velvety sauce.

☞ 2. Rinse the pasta if you're making a cold salad.

First off, the cool water will chill it off and so keep the flavors in the dressing from volatilizing with the heat. Second, the pasta will hold together better in the dressing without tearing and sharding.

☞ 3. Rinse the pasta if you're making a pasta casserole.

Torn lasagna noodles or giant shells are no one's idea of a dinner. And don't worry about the sauce sticking to the noodles. It's going to be held in place by all that luscious cheese you've got in the casserole.

PASTA SALAD WITH PESTO VINAIGRETTE

4 main-course servings, more for a side dish

This is a summer staple because it's so very light and bright in its flavors. A traditional pesto is made with pine nuts and lots of oil—but we've morphed the proportions a bit to make this one more like a dressing, and we use almonds for a lighter, sweeter taste, better against the slightly acidic pop of those tomatoes. Heck, it's a good fit even in the winter, when you're yearning for a spark of summer.

12 ounces dried ziti, rigatoni, roteli, or other medium
　　pasta shape
1 cup packed basil leaves
¼ cup olive oil, the most fragrant you
　　can comfortably afford
1 ounce Parmigiano-Reggiano, finely
　　grated (that is, ¼ cup)
3 tablespoons sliced almonds
1 tablespoon white wine vinegar
1 medium garlic clove, slivered
¼ teaspoon salt
¼ teaspoon freshly ground black pepper
2 cups grape or cherry tomatoes, quartered
1 medium cucumber, peeled, halved lengthwise, seeded, and
　　chopped (see page 192, step 2 for a fuller explanation)

1. Bring a large pot of water to a boil over high heat, at least 3 quarts of water. Dump in the pasta, then stir several times during the first 3 minutes of cooking to ensure it doesn't stick. Continue boiling until tender. The only way to know is to taste one. Try it at 4 minutes and see where you are. Maybe a couple of minutes more?

2. Drain the pasta in a colander set in the sink, then rinse it well with cool water. Set aside to drain more.

3. Stem the basil leaves of any woody ends, then wash them thoroughly under cool water to remove any dirt and grit. Do not dry the leaves. Place them in a large food processor fitted with the chopping blade.

4. Add the olive oil, cheese, almonds, vinegar, garlic, salt, and pepper. Do not even think about using canned Parmesan cheese. Buy a little block of the real thing and grate it yourself on a cheese plane or through the small holes of a box grater.

5. Pulse the food processor a few times, then scrape down the inside of the canister with a rubber spatula and process to a grainy paste. Check for salt—it may need a little more. But remember that you can also salt individual servings later.

6. Pour the cooked pasta into a big serving bowl. Add the tomatoes and cucumber. Scrape the pesto dressing on top and toss well, coating everything. Serve at once or cover and refrigerate for up to 1 day, tossing again before serving.

GELATIN IS MADE FROM HORSE HOOVES.

JUST BECAUSE IT'S GROSS DOESN'T MEAN IT'S TRUE.

Southerners have a hard-and-fast rule: if the Jell-O has marshmallows, it's a dessert. If it doesn't, it's a salad. Both marshmallows and Jell-O are made with gelatin. But gelatin is not made from horse hooves. Or hooves of any sort.

Hooves are made from keratin, a fibrous protein found in your own hair and fingernails. Put simply, keratin does not gel when boiled.

Gelatin is made from the partial hydrolysis of collagen, the most common protein in vertebrates, found mostly in their connective tissues, tendons, skin, and bones. It is to animals what cellulose is to plants.

If you make a pot of chicken soup, the collagen will leak out of all the connective tissue and skin, thereby turning the soup rich and luscious—and a solid quivering mass of gelled poultry goodness after it's been refrigerated.

Collagen is also the sticky lusciousness that makes short ribs and oxtails so darn irresistible in a braise. It's layered thick in hams, chicken thighs, pork shoulders, lamb chops, and briskets—all the good stuff. And it's so necessary for human life that some researchers believe it is the single reason humans first began eating meat.

Since most of the collagen-rich connective tissue and tendons in meat stays put in the various cuts for sale at the market, what's left for gelatin production is mostly the excess skin from mammals after butchering.

The hides are cut into little bits, cleansed of impurities, dehaired, then soaked in lime for up to a month. The bits are then given a bath in sulfuric acid, which transforms the collagen-rich bits into a gelatin-like substance. Everything's then given a good rinse and cooked until the collagen melts.

Finally, there's every kind of filtering, evaporating, chilling, and crushing, all until what's left are those little granules. Collagen has now been changed chemically and physically into gelatin. Yes, there are gelatins made from kosher animals. And yes, there are gelatins made from fish bones. But there are no plant-based gelatins. You can't get blood *or collagen* from a turnip. If you eat gelatin, you have blood on your hands, just not hooves.

That said, there are a few thickening agents from plants—guar gum, carrageenan, or agar agar, to name three. But these are not gelatins. They're gummy, sticky compounds that can hold certain liquids in suspension. They can make low-fat ice cream creamier. But they are not gelatins in the true sense of the word.

A POTATO DROPPED INTO SOUP WILL ABSORB ANY EXCESS SALT.

NOT IN THE WAYS YOU THINK.

Salty soup apparently is every cook's bane. That heavy pour at the beginning, that slowly evaporating liquid level—and soon enough, the Dead Sea in a dish.

For generations, the answer has been the lowly spud. Cut it into a few rounds—many food writers say to peel it first for more salt absorption—and then drop it in the simmering vat.

Later, they advise you to take the slices out and taste one. See, it's pretty darn salty. It must have removed some of the salt from the soup.

It did—but it didn't fix the soup.

First off, potatoes absorb liquids. So lobbing spud rounds into the pot will remove some of the liquid, which indeed has dissolved salt in it. Yes, the overall salt level in the pot has decreased—but so has the overall liquid level. Which means you've been left with about the same ratio of salt to water as you began with. And given that the soup has been bubbling away as the potatoes got tender, there may even be a higher salt concentration in the pot. Welcome back to the Dead Sea.

And second, your taste acclimates quickly to saltiness. You

munch the potato, notice its briny qualities, and then sip the soup. Less there, you think—although not actually.

You might as well have dropped a sponge in the soup. It, too, would have absorbed salty water. Then you could have poured in some more broth, thus dropping the overall salt ratio. Voilà, fixed soup.

You could also try adding a little sugar to that saline-doped pot. The enhanced sweetness can balance the salty taste. There won't actually *be* less salt, but you may taste less.

On that note, another reason for the potato-to-the-rescue myth may be the nature of potatoes themselves. They're sweet, full of carbs (a.k.a. sugars)—which can then balance some of the saltiness. It won't cure what's in the pot, but you can fake yourself out.

Or try dropping in a bunch of dried pasta. The spaghetti or ziti will also absorb salty liquid—although in the same ratio as those spuds. Soon enough, those noodles will soak a lot of the liquid out of the pot, enough so that you can pour in more broth and start again without such a heavy pour of salt at the start.

Which is really the only way to cure a salty soup. Stop pouring in salt. Start measuring.

When you're making soup, go ahead and add a little salt at the beginning—perhaps ½ teaspoon for four servings. It will nudge some of the vegetables and the meat in the mix to release their pent-up liquids. The broth will get tastier. The soup, more flavorful. Then once the whole thing is ready to eat, dish it up into bowls and bring a little crunchy sea salt to the table. Everyone can sprinkle till their heart's content.

EATING CARROTS IMPROVES YOUR EYESIGHT.

A LITTLE "YES" BUT MOSTLY "NO."

Not the way your grandmother meant it. Not when she tried to foist those carrot sticks onto you when all you wanted was a candy bar.

Still, she got something right. Carrots are rich in vitamin A, which the digestive tract converts into *retinol,* a vitamin A storage vehicle, which can then be further transformed into *retinal,* a light-absorbing molecule required by the eyes for both low-light and color vision.

Our main source of vitamin A is beta-carotene and other carotinoids, found in (yes) carrots but lots of other fruits and vegetables like sweet potatoes, any orange-fleshed winter squash, collard greens, kale, spinach, mangoes, and papayas.

A diet rich in good sources of vitamin A can help *maintain* your current eyesight, but it's not cheap lasic. Your eyes won't get better. Besides, if you have a pronounced deficiency of vitamin A, you'll also have had lots of other symptoms, like hair loss and acute bone pain.

Still, vitamin A deficiencies are a stubborn, global problem, especially in developing countries. Children do end up blind. You need that vitamin A at a very early age. Getting it as a teenager is mostly getting it too late.

In fact, the benefits of vitamin A consumption may fall off with age. The Blue Mountains study, a major Australian study conducted in the late 1990s, explored the link between increased dietary vitamin A intake and the deterioration of night vision in older adults. The participants ate more carrots—just as their grandmothers had told them to—but there was no measurable improvement in their sight problems.

Furthermore, eating lots of carrots can have a secondary, probably unwanted effect. Those beta-carotenes have pigment dyes. Eat enough and you'll turn orange, as if you used a spray-on tanning cream.

In truth, you won't have any deficiency if you eat a balanced diet. Or drink milk. Most milk sold in the United States is fortified with vitamin A.

With one problem: vitamin A is *fat*-soluble. So fortified fat-free milk will do you little good on the vitamin A front. Unless you're drinking it alongside a bowl of buttered carrots.

CARROT GINGER SOUP

8 servings, more with a salad on the side

You may not see better after eating this soup, but your insides will almost certainly feel better! There's a lot of good nutrition here—and a lot of fine flavors, particularly that warm ginger which is both spiky and soothing, a miracle combination. If you want to make this a vegetarian meal, substitute vegetable broth for the chicken, but understand that some canned vegetable broth is truly insipid, little more than what we call *onion water.* Do a taste test among brands to find one that is right for you.

2 tablespoons peanut oil (see page 78) or olive oil
1 small yellow onion, chopped
¼ cup fresh ginger, peeled and minced,
   or jarred minced ginger
2 medium garlic cloves, minced
½ cup dry white wine or dry vermouth
2 pounds peeled carrots, sliced into ½-inch rounds
1 quart canned, fat-free, reduced-sodium chicken broth
½ teaspoon salt
½ teaspoon freshly ground black pepper
½ teaspoon ground cinnamon
½ cup plain Greek-style yogurt

1. Heat a large pot over medium heat, then swirl in the oil. Add the onion and cook, stirring often, until translucent, about 4 minutes.

2. Stir in the ginger and garlic and continue cooking for about 30 seconds, just enough to release some of their essential oils.

3. Pour in the white wine or vermouth. As it comes to a simmer, stir the pot several times to make sure any onion or garlic has come loose from the bottom.

4. Dump in all the carrots. Stir them around for a minute, then add the broth, salt, pepper, and cinnamon. Stir well and bring to a full, bubbling simmer over medium-high heat.

5. Cover the pot, reduce the heat to low, and simmer until the carrots are tender when poked with a fork, stirring once in a while, about 30 minutes. Set the pot off the heat for a few minutes to cool down.

6. Now purée it. You've got several options. You can use an immersion blender right in the pot, stirring it around to make sure everything on the bottom comes in contact with its blades. Or pour the soup in batches into a large blender and give it a whir. However, remove the center knob in the lid so that the pressure doesn't build up and spew the hot soup all over your kitchen. Cover that opening with a clean kitchen towel and blend until smooth. Once done, pour the purée back into the pot.

7. Set the thick, smooth soup over low heat and stir in the yogurt until smooth. Keep the pot over the heat a minute or so, just to heat the soup back up. Now it's ready to serve.

8

DOCTORS ARE NEVER WRONG
Myths Born of Nutrition Fads

There's just something about a lab coat. You can't wear one without knowing what you're talking about, right?

Unfortunately, all is not well in the land of syringes and catheters. Partly because the possibility of fame and fortune has gotten cloaked in that lab coat, too.

Over the past couple of decades, we've been barraged with slipshod, pseudo-medical nutrition myths, most trying to crest a fad—*Eat no fat! Eat more fat! Eat this! Don't eat that!*—all in the hopes of a quick buck. We've already run into a couple of these sorts of myths under other headings—like that *drink red wine for your health* blather or that BS about calorie-negative foods. But there are more to come. More every day, it seems.

In the end, we can't solve the problem of the lab coat as a masquerade costume. But we can dispense with some of the more pernicious myths that continue to make the circuit, many of them trying to scare us into signing up for a monthly credit card deduction so we can follow some "revolutionary" plan. If it seems to good to be true, it probably is. By the way, the same goes for the instant bliss you're supposed to get from marrying someone in a lab coat.

YOU CRAVE SUGAR, FAT, AND SALT BECAUSE YOU'RE ADDICTED TO THEM.

AND THERE'S ALSO A DISTURBANCE IN THE FORCE.

Actually, you like these things because they make food taste good. You may even want them. Bad. But it's doubtful that you're addicted to them. In truth, the term "addiction" is too often applied to behavior that does not fall under the strict definition of the word. We've heard far too much about porn "addictions," social-media "addictions," and (yes) food "addictions."

An addiction is a biochemical miswiring—or even a long-term rewiring. It results in certain potentially fatal behaviors like the willingness to risk life and limb to fulfill soul-rattling cravings. An addict *cannot* (not "will not") abstain from or even recognize the behavorial problems.

It is *not* the same thing as a dependency. Yes, dependencies can be pitched pretty high. Just think of that freshman crush in college. Or butter pecan ice cream. And yes, some dependencies can result in cravings. But those cravings rarely escalate to the burn-everything-down-to-get-the-fix behavior that comes from an addiction. And if they do, there are most likely other psychological issues at play. Put simply, addictions result in cravings, but most cravings are not the result of addictions.

Most cravings—including the ones for ice cream—are emotional dependencies, a sort of mind-itch, desires run amok. You *will not* stop eating that ice cream—that behavior is nothing to dismiss out of hand. But you *can* stop eating it, if the motivation's right.

Other cravings cross a line to become dire, psychological, and even physical torments. The body convulses; the mind is consumed. Addiction.

Yes, the former, lesser cravings can lead to the latter, but not necessarily—and less often than you'd think. When it comes to food, there's credible evidence of sharp dependencies but almost none of addiction, with the exception of rare cases where food cravings and mental illness fuse.

We were once at a schmancy wedding, the sort where you could eat nonstop for eight hours straight. At the end of the gorge-fest, they wheeled out a chocolate fountain. Everyone was already beyond well fed, but boy, did they dive for that thing! You've never seen so many sharp elbows.

Were these people addicted to chocolate? No. But some may have had a bit of a dependency. Food cravings may make people go nuts; but battling addiction ends in actual, physical withdrawal. Give up chocolate and you may be irritable for a couple of days but you will not be on the floor, vomiting and hallucinating.

Just to be clear, we're talking about food here, not about ethanol and its addiction—a.k.a. alcoholism. Ethanol is a brain-reengineering drug. People do present the classic signs of addiction in and out of detox.

And that's not to say that food cravings have no effect on the brain. In fact, they intensify based on the specificity of the imagined pleasure. If you think *chocolate,* not much will probably happen. Oh, maybe a little brain itch, but not much else. But if you think *a ripe sweet strawberry dipped in warm milk chocolate,* the brain itch gets more intense. The more specific the image, the more mental space it eats up. One recent study showed that people who imagined a specific chocolate dessert even had less *vocabulary* at the ready. The image actually took up cognitive space. Maybe that's why so many of us fall slack-jawed in front of the ice cream case at the supermarket.

IT'S BETTER TO EAT SEVERAL SMALL MEALS A DAY, RATHER THAN THREE LARGE ONES.

THAT PATENT IS STILL PENDING.

A couple of years ago, several nutrition pundits made the rounds, suggesting that people who nibbled their food in many small courses during the day were thinner and healthier than us three-square types.

To debunk this, we need to bring in the heavy guns: Einstein. Particularly, his theory on the conservation of mass and energy, the bedrock of modern physics.

In the end, it doesn't matter whether you eat your food in tiny bites or one big gulp. What you eat brings along its calories. And a calorie is a calorie—that is, a unit of energy. Unless you've been able to reconfigure time and space, the calories you consume don't alter based on when you swallow them, no matter if they're on one enormous platter downed in a ten-minute snarf or on a dozen niggling plates pecked at over the course of the day.

A calorie measures the amount of energy required to raise the temperature of one gram of water (.035 ounce, less than ¼ teaspoon) 1°C (that is, about 1.8°F). Back in the day, chemists put a piece of food in a sealed chamber, surrounded the chamber with water, burned the food to ashes, and measured how much the water temperature increased.

These days, calories measure how much energy food yields once your body metabolizes it: as stamina, as tissue, as bone, as endocrine secretions, as glucose for the brain, as fat stores, as digestive elimination.

Problem is, when we now talk about dietary calories, we're actually talking about kilocalories (that is, 1,000 calories). We say 1% milk has 102 calories per cup; we mean it has 102 kilocalories per cup—or 102,000 calories. As with an overly inflated currency, we've lopped off the zeroes and labeled the result *calories.*

Still, it doesn't matter how you take them in. If all you eat today is six hundred calories, no matter in one plateful or three, you're probably going to lose weight. And if you down four thousand calories today, no matter if you nibble them or wolf them down, you're going to gain weight—unless you run lots of marathons.

So what happened to the studies that supposedly backed up these nutrition pundits? As is too often the case, they were conducted without proper controls. Specifically: the three-squarers *understated* the number of snacks they ate every day. All the participants were fed their meals by the research technicians and given equivalent amounts to eat during the day, no matter in many plates or few. But then the participants were free to go their merry ways, back to work or home; and the three-squarers snuck snacks. So the amount of calories consumed was off. Naturally the nibblers didn't feel the urge to snack because another meal was coming very soon and so lost pounds in the long run.

And right there may be the studies' one benefit: eating many smaller meals cuts down on snacking. And snacking is the problem, the point where we three-squarers fall down. From breakfast to lunch, there's a four- or five-hour gap. We can mostly make it. But from lunch to dinner, there's sometimes an eight-hour gap. It's too long; we get hungry, need to snack. And so we become both nibblers and snarfers all in one day.

Our best advice is to cut out the mindless nibbling and plan on some apple and cheddar at about 4:00 p.m. Don't sneak—have a little something intentionally in the long break before dinner. But remember: a calorie is a calorie, no matter when you eat it. If you want to lose weight, eat less and move more. We could put the entire diet industry out of business with that one sentence.

EATING AT NIGHT MAKES YOU GAIN WEIGHT.

TOO BAD THEY DUMPED LOGIC AS A COLLEGE REQUIREMENT.

We're back to Einstein: a calorie is a calorie. It doesn't morph into something else late in the evening like a werewolf during a full moon. Eating more calories than you burn off causes weight gain. It's that simple.

This myth about eating at night no doubt stems from the idea that if you consume calories at night, you're probably sitting on your duff, watching TV, not working them off.

However, you never work off the calories you just consumed. You can go out for lunch and chow down on an iceberg wedge with blue cheese dressing, a triple decker cheeseburger, a mound of fries, a couple of beers, and a chocolate sundae, then hit the gym in a fit of guilt and run on the treadmill like mad. But don't kid yourself: you're not burning off your lunch. You're burning off the calories you took in over the past several days. Much of the food you had at lunch hasn't even left your stomach yet. (Which is one of the reasons you're starting to feel a little queasy on the treadmill.) And some of that food may not even be gone by the time you sit down to dinner that evening.

When you work off the calories is of far less importance than the fact *that* you work them off. But that doesn't mean eating late at night is necessarily okay. Because, by and large, you're not being a Spaniard: dinner at midnight. Instead, you're probably snacking.

Whenever you eat, endorphins get released in your brain. You get mellow and content. Soon, you can start medicating with snacks every evening to release those pleasure chemicals. And then it all becomes a self-perpetuating cycle, a dependency: you've had a hard day, you want to relax, you snack after dinner, you feel better, you eat more, and so on.

You might consider doing something else to release those very same endorphins. Like running on a treadmill.

WHAT YOU LIKE TO EAT IS PART OF YOUR GENETIC MAKEUP.

THE TRUTH IS OFTEN BETTER— AND SOMETIMES MEANER.

An increasing body of evidence suggests that you don't like Brussels sprouts, not because of your parents' genes, but because of your parents themselves.

As babies, we haven't fully developed our communication skills. We don't talk all that much, but we've got mad nonverbal skills. Tone of voice, bodily cues—these are our bailiwicks. Most development psychologists believe that as we become increasingly verbal, we lose many of these more native talents. Which is why most marriages devolve into a constant refrain of "Are you mad at me?"

So let's say you're an infant just starting solid foods. Your mom's holding up a little jar: Puréed Brussels Sprouts. But you're a baby; you can't read the label or even necessarily distinguish the jar's contents by color. Nonetheless, your mother is going on and on about how much you're going to love the green mush—even though it nauseates her. You have no idea what she's saying, but you can read her like a book. The way one corner of her mouth is turned down a little.

That slight quaver in her tone. The way her eyes dart back and forth. And many more cues we've since forgotten how to see.

She's hesitant; you're instantly afraid. You start bawling as the green puke nears your mouth. A few more times and the spoon becomes associated with Mom's grimace. And thirty years later, it's the same thing. "Oh, right, you've never liked Brussels sprouts, but are you mad at me?"

Our scenario is fully supported by research from David Benton at Swansea University. He's found that infants' tastes are primarily based on their parents' *attitudes*. Infants from environments with a greater, more open range of food choices have more open palates and fewer dislikes. By contrast, infants from environments with far few choices and pronounced food antipathies have more closed palates. Indeed, the determining factor in the closed environments apparently was fear—that is, the parents' fear of types of food—or even of food itself. That fear, even if expressed nonverbally, even unconsciously, directly affected the development of the infants' tastes.

The good news is that your palate is not set even now. The more you're exposed to certain foods, the more you'll like them. So the old saw is right: don't try it once; try it several times.

Research also shows that people who cook their own meals have a wider palate range. So if you find yourself eating a very narrow swath of foods, try cooking more. Your palate will soon expand. You'll find yourself liking more things. Maybe even Brussels sprouts. Just not the puréed ones. Some horrors are still unspeakable.

YOU CAN NEVER EAT ENOUGH FIBER.

TOO MUCH OF A GOOD THING IS JUST TOO MUCH.

No doubt, fiber is beneficial. In fact, we need both kinds: soluble and insoluble. One ultimately dissolves in water (think oranges and broccoli); one never will (think corn hulls).

True enough, most of us don't eat enough of either. On average, we Americans eat less than half of what we need every day. So the inevitable happens: a marketing plan. We need something, manufacturers hear about it, they add lots of it to their products, they get a heavy shot of boosterism, and we're soon quaffing orange juice with added fiber—despite the fact that oranges by themselves are a great source of fiber.

Then there's this: the fiber that's added to many processed foods—mostly for the call-out on the label—is so processed, its health benefits are compromised. For example:

☞ **Inulin, a.k.a. chickory-root extract.**
It's also a fat-replacer. It encourages good bacteria in your gut. But you'd need to eat so much to get the good effect that you'd end up on the toilet all day long.

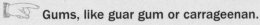 **Gums, like guar gum or carrageenan.**

These are added as thickeners, particularly in low-fat or fat-free products. In very large amounts, they can reduce bad cholesterol and regulate blood sugar levels. But to reap the digestive benefits, you'd need enough to send you to the toilet all day long.

Processed cellulose.

It's from plant cell walls and is found in low-carb everything. It's great for the digestive tract, but it's got a quick tipping point. Eat enough and you'll be on the . . . you get the point.

Sure, these processed fiber alternatives can help move things along down there. But not as well as, oh, a bowl of oatmeal. Or a bean salad. Or green beans. Or any hard winter squash. Or cherries. Or berries. Or just about any fruit or vegetable you can name. Even spuds are full of fiber!

All of these foods contain a mix of the various kinds of soluble and insoluble fiber, each with its unique benefit to and use in the body. What's more, many experts think it's not only the fiber that makes you healthy but all the nutrients that travel with it. Foods doped with so-called *added fiber* most often have only one kind of fiber, stripped of its bounty of nutrients—and so again may not be as beneficial as, oh, an apple.

Still, don't go nuts with bean salad or oatmeal. Excessive fiber intake—more than 50 grams a day—can lead to fluid imbalances (namely, dehydration since fiber absorbs liquid) and certain mineral deficiencies because the excess bulk washes everything right out of you. And intriguingly, way too much fiber can lead to intestinal obstructions, which will probably send you right to surgery. You'll get cleaned out, just not in the way you want to.

So have a handful of cherries. Or some raspberries. Or try the broccoli, even with some melted butter. Better that than industrially created fiber that does nothing except keep you on the . . . right, you got it.

FRENCH WOMEN DON'T GET FAT.

YEAH, RIGHT.

Despite claims to the contrary, the obesity epidemic is coming to France. Fast. As of 2007, 42 percent of the French were not just overweight but obese. While that figure pales in comparison to statistics for the United States (about 65 percent of Americans are not just overweight but obese), the French are expected to catch up by 2020.

To be sure, those obesity stats are not as dire in certain chic Parisian arrondissements. But the people there are slim and trim in the same way that they are on Manhattan's Upper East Side or in Hollywood: they eat smaller portions of higher-quality food, they go to the gym frequently, and many have been trimmed by the surgeon's knife.

For the rest of France, it's the same there as here: an increasingly processed diet, a lack of exercise, a dependence on high-fat restaurant fare, a blinding whirlwind of carb-heavy snack foods, and a backlash against the overeating warnings being dispensed by the government.

Of course, there's always been the so-called *French paradox*: the notion that these people eat a cream-laden, cheese-filled diet and yet remain trim. The average French person eats 171 grams of fat a day; the average American, about 157. Yet the

French suffer far fewer deaths from coronary heart disease every year.

There have been a variety of explanations: genetics, red wine consumption (the French beat us there), fish consumption (the French also beat us there), saturated fat consumption (oddly, the French beat us there, too), and vegetable oil consumption (finally, a category we win). But even these differences have fallen to naught within the last few years as our two countries have homogenized and are now plagued by the same epidemic. Indeed, discovering *a* cause among myriad variables may be an exercise in futility.

But don't be fooled. That recent best-seller on skinny French women claimed to help you lose weight by making you drink warm leek water for a couple of days—and then had the Gallic gall to proffer it as an entrée into some French lifestyle that keeps you trim. Listen, anybody would be skinny quaffing leek water!

French people do get fat. And are getting fatter every day.

LENTILS AUX LARDONS

4 hearty servings

Or *lentils with bacon.* But no matter what you call it, it represents the best way to stay trim: to search for more satiety in every bite of food you eat. And there, the French have us beat, given the sheer range of textures and flavors in most of their classic dishes. This one's a riff on a bistro favorite, with lentils filling in for the usual greens, an even more satisfying meal bite for bite.

1½ cups green lentils, sometimes called French lentils, *picked over for any little stones or pebbles (do not use brown or soup lentils)*
½ pound slab bacon, diced
1 very small red onion, diced
2 large celery ribs, sliced lengthwise and then diced
2 large carrots, grated through the large holes of a box grater
¼ cup white wine vinegar
2 teaspoons Dijon mustard
2 teaspoons Worcestershire sauce
1 teaspoon honey
½ teaspoon freshly ground black pepper
4 large eggs

1. Put the lentils in a large saucepan, then fill it with cool water until the water stands about 3 inches over the lentils. Set the pot over high heat and bring to a boil, stirring occasionally. Reduce the heat to medium and simmer, uncovered, until the lentils are just tender, 10 to 15 minutes. The time differential has to do with how much residual moisture those little pulses have in them after sitting on the shelf. The only real way to tell if they're done is to taste one or two. Drain the lentils in a small-holed colander or a fine-mesh sieve set in the sink. Rinse with cool water to bring down their temperature and stop the cooking. Transfer the lentils to a large bowl.

2. Place the bacon bits in a large skillet set over medium heat. Cook, stirring often, until crisp. Use a slotted spoon to transfer the bacon bits to the bowl with the lentils, leaving the grease behind in the skillet.

3. Set the skillet back over medium heat and add the onion, celery, and carrots. Cook, stirring often, until the onion begins to go translucent, about 4 minutes.

4. Stir in the vinegar, mustard, Worcestershire sauce, and honey. As the liquid boils, scrape up any browned bits across the skillet's bottom. Simmer for about 20 seconds, until a little reduced; then scrape the contents of the skillet into the bowl with the lentils and bacon. Add the pepper, stir well, and set aside.

5. Bring a large pot of water to a boil over high heat. Reduce the heat to the lowest setting possible, so the water barely moves. Crack 1 egg into a little bowl or custard cup, then slip it into the water. Repeat quickly with the other 3 eggs.

6. Cover the pot and set it aside off the heat for 4 minutes. Meanwhile, divide the lentil salad among four serving plates.

7. Use a slotted spoon to scoop up the eggs from the pot, draining them a bit before setting one by one on top of their own salads. To eat the salad, let the yolk run down into the lentils, thereby creating a ridiculously great dressing with those bacon drippings and the vinegar. Serve with a crunchy baguette.

MYTH #79

SATURATED FAT IS A NO-NO.

THANK GOD, NO.

This is the first myth in a chain of three on dietary fats. This one actually came about because of the potentially dunderheaded notion that saturated fat raises blood cholesterol. *Toss out the butter, get rid of the steaks,* the pundits say. Such advice itself may well be wrong.

First, there is no one thing called *saturated fat.* Instead, it's a category that includes many fats, all of them acids: stearic acid, lauric acid, palmitic acid, myristic acid, and others.

The body deals with them in different ways. For example, palmitic acid, one of the fats in lots of dairy and some meat, can be trouble in the blood—as you'd expect from something used to make napalm. However, if consumed in combination with linoleic acid, a fatty acid found in some fish and plants, palmitic acid has been shown actually to reduce the LDL count (the "bad" cholesterol number). So butter that salmon!

Stearic acid appears to be even better. It's found in beef, dairy, poultry, coconut, and even chocolate, particularly cocoa. It leaves the "bad" LDL count unchanged while raising the "good" HDL number—mostly because a healthy body converts stearic acid into oleic acid, a monounsaturated fat.

What's more, there is no credible link between the consumption of saturated fats and the risk of coronary disease. One eight-year study from the Women's Health Initiative, called *The Nurses' Health Study*, followed 49,000 post–menopausal American women. Shifting the ratio between saturated and unsaturated fats in their diets had *no* appreciable effect on their risk. However, remember this: the overall number of *calories* wasn't changed, just the ratio among the fats. This study is not an excuse to eat half a pound of bacon for breakfast!

Other studies have come to similar conclusions. One found that saturated fats raise the "good" numbers higher than they raise the bad numbers, thus, improving the overall ratio. Another found that diets high in saturated fats result in lower numbers for the sticky, clogging LDL.

But if there's an open road to culinary redemption for bad-mouthed foods, it's still barricaded by some misguided members of the medical community. The new USDA food pyramid advises you to eat less meat, mostly because of stated fears of saturated fat. However, that same pyramid also advises higher dairy consumption. And dairy products are high in saturated fat!

Yes, there is evidence linking colon cancer with a meat-heavy diet. Meat is also calorie dense. And it's expensive. And it's hard on the planet to raise the stuff. There *are* good reasons for limiting the amount of meat you eat.

But *cutting down* is not *cutting out*. A sensibly sized steak now and then is hard to beat—and even better without a big heaping side dish of guilt and fear.

LARD IS A SATURATED FAT.

PROBABLY "YES" IN A STORE, MAYBE "NO" ON YOUR STOVE.

To debunk this, we first have to talk about dietary fats themselves. There are two categories, both acids, both *lipids:* saturated and unsaturated fat. That second category is itself divided in two: monounsaturated and polyunsaturated. Despite such divisions, all dietary fats look the same: like a capital *E* turned on its side, the long line on top with three legs dangling down. That long line is a glycerin chain, a glycerol. From it hang the lipids (or fatty acids), made up of various organic molecules, some bonded tightly together, some a little freer.

If there's no freedom in the chain, the fat is stiff—and thus said to be *saturated*. If there's any freedom at all, even the tiniest bit, the fat is said to be *unsaturated*. You can see how the term can be misleading—it sounds as if *unsaturated* means total freedom, although it's merely a matter of degree. If the chain dangles in just one place, it's called *monounsaturated*. And if it dangles in several, it's *polyunsaturated*.

Think of it this way: let's say we needed to make a line of people—and all we had on hand were Presbyterians. They wouldn't dandle. Nor loll about. They'd stand upright. Things would be in order. And thus saturated.

Then we stick a Unitarian in the line. Suddenly, those Calvinists sway! Well, not a lot. Just at one point, right at the Unitarian. The line is now *monounsaturated*.

Then we go wild and put two Unitarians in the line. Wow, anarchy. Well, not really. Most of the Presbyterians are still pretty stiff. But there are two places where the line dandles. That is, multiple points. Thus, it's *polyunsaturated*. A Presbyterian might even smile, if things got really out of control.

All dietary fats contain all three kinds of chains. We only call a fat saturated or monounsaturated or polyunsaturated based on which predominates in the bigger, greasier mix. For example, we call olive oil a monounsaturated fat; however, on average it's made up of 74 percent monounsaturated fat, 13 percent saturated fat, and 8 percent polyunsaturated fat. (Proprietal blends will have varying numbers, most fairly in line with this generalization.) We also call peanut oil a monounsaturated fat; but it's actually 46 percent monounsaturated fat, 32 percent polyunsaturated fat, and 17 percent saturated fat.

So now to lard at long last. It's 45 percent monounsaturated fat, 40 percent saturated fat, and 11 percent polyunsaturated fat. Thus, lard is a monounsaturated fat. Sort of like olive oil. But way more Faulknerian.

Now for the bad news. Most of the lard in our supermarkets has been hydrogenated to make it shelf-stable. It's loaded with trans-fats, a real evil we'll meet in the next myth. Our solution? Render your own lard and keep it in the freezer, no hydrogenation necessary. But we'll save that for another day (and another book).

Bottom line: all fat is high in calories, is tasty, and should be treated with respect. So have some home-rendered lard, especially in piecrusts or on sautéed greens. It's good for you. It may even get you to reread Faulkner.

WALNUT PIE WITH A LARD CRUST

Makes one 9-inch pie that'll feed about 6 people

Okay, you don't have to use lard. And we certainly don't recommend the trans-fat laden, shelf-stable stuff. But at your local farmers' market, you can often find a steady supply of real lard, which will add a savory ping to this pie. If you still don't want to go the distance, substitute half trans-fat-free shortening and half cold butter for the crust's lard.

$1\frac{1}{3}$ *cups all-purpose flour, plus more for dusting your work surface*

$\frac{1}{4}$ *cup plus 2 teaspoons granulated white sugar*

$\frac{1}{2}$ *teaspoon salt*

8 tablespoons ($\frac{1}{2}$ cup) lard, cut into small pieces

3 to 5 tablespoons iced water

1 teaspoon cider vinegar

3 large eggs

1 cup maple syrup, preferably Grade
    A Dark Amber or Grade B
¾ cup packed dark brown sugar
2 tablespoons unsalted butter, melted and cooled
1 tablespoon vanilla extract
3 cups walnut pieces

1. Position the rack in the oven's center and heat the oven to 350°F.

2. Use a fork to mix the flour, 2 teaspoons sugar, and ¼ teaspoon salt in a big bowl. Cut in the lard, using either a pastry cutter or fork. Press the flour mixture through the fat, repeatedly scraping off the tines until the whole thing resembles coarse sand, the fat grains tiny and coated in flour.

3. Sprinkle 3 tablespoons iced water and the vinegar over the flour. Stir with a fork, then start adding more water in dribs and drabs until you can ball the whole thing up, the dough coherent and uniform. But don't add too much water. Be judicious.

4. Sprinkle some water across your work surface, then lay a large piece of wax paper on top of it. The water will hold the wax paper. Dust it with flour. Drop the dough ball in the center and press it out until it's a round about ½ inch thick. Dust it with flour, too. Take a rolling pin and roll the dough into a circle about 11 inches wide. Add a little more flour if it sticks at all. Pick up the wax paper sheet with the dough on it and turn it upside down in a 9-inch pie plate. Press the dough into place and peel off the wax paper. Shape it to the pie plate and trim off the excess at the rim. Press the tines of a fork repeatedly around the rim to give it a decorative edge.

5. Whisk the eggs, maple syrup, brown sugar, melted butter, vanilla, the remaining ¼ cup white sugar, and the remaining ¼ teaspoon salt in a clean bowl until smooth, no bits of egg loose in the mixture. And don't you dare use anything except real maple syrup.

6. Stir in the walnut pieces, then pour this filling into the piecrust. Place in the oven and bake until the filling is puffed and brown, until it gives a slight jiggle when the side of the pie plate is tapped, about 55 minutes. Cool on a wire rack for at least 1 hour before slicing into wedges to serve.

MARGARINE IS BETTER FOR YOU THAN BUTTER.

SAY IT AIN'T SO!

We hate to tell you, but Eleanor Roosevelt was wrong. Did you know she hocked Good Luck margarine in the late '50s, long after the war? Look it up on YouTube. Our favorite part of the commercial is when the announcer says that Good Luck is "light in flavor, light on the tongue, and leaves no oily aftertaste."

Back in Eleanor's day, margarine was sold as a health product, a claim that's a little hard to swallow. After all, almost all fat has a similar amount of calories: about 120 per tablespoon.

Butter has slightly fewer, since it also has milk solids in the mix. Yes, butter has saturated fats. We've been over those. Mostly, it has great taste.

Margarine? About the same calories as butter, slightly fewer than liquid fats, mostly because of the air whipped into the mix. It apparently once had an oily aftertaste, but they've taken care of that. Still, there's something worse in many margarines: trans fats, an industrial by-product, made when hydrogen is whipped into fat. Why would anyone want to do that? So the fat becomes shelf stable, doesn't go rancid for months, and even holds its shape longer.

Trans fats are bad all around. The same *Nurses' Health Study* about cholesterol, the one that found that changing the ratio of saturated to unsaturated fats had no effect on heart attack risks, also showed that including trans fats in the mix significantly raised the risk rate.

Until the mid-'60s, margarine was so hydrogenated, so stuffed with trans fats, that it could be molded into sticks so people could tear their toast with it right out of the fridge, just like with butter.

Then everyone got into spreadability. So manufacturers started hydrogenating it less and adding polyunsaturated oils, all in the name of getting it to smear from the tubs. So yes, modern margarines have fewer trans fats than their predecessors. But *fewer* is the operative word.

And yes, there are now trans-fat-free margarines on the market. Problem is, all these modern concoctions have less and less flavor. And studies show that monochromatic, blander food encourages overeating as the body misses key signals to satiety.

And just for the record, butter does indeed have some naturally occurring trans fats. But almost nil. About 0.39 grams (or 0.014 ounces) per tablespoon.

Even so, why wouldn't you go with the choice that tastes better? Butter, we assure you, has never had an oily aftertaste. You'll be satisfied sooner. Sorry, Eleanor.

FRIED FOODS CAN'T BE HEALTHY.

DO YOU ALSO HAVE TICKETS FOR THE NEXT TRAIN TO BERMUDA?

Proper frying is a thing of beauty. Batter up a chicken leg or a mushroom, then drop it into hot oil. The moisture in the coating instantly starts to vaporize; the oil froths as that moisture boils away. Wait the right amount of time and take the food out. The coating is crunchy because it's dehydrated, having expanded and then hardened into a web of shards and threads.

In fact, there can be very little added oil in the final product. Thus, fried foods need not be unhealthy, just for being fried. Problem is, they have to be fried right. Otherwise, yes, they're not healthy at all. Everyone's had a gummy, greasy piece of fried chicken. It's bad—and bad for you. But there are four ways to circumvent the problem:

 The oil has to be hot.

At 375°F, to be exact. If it's cooler, the famed moisture burst won't happen quickly enough and the oil will begin to invade the food before the coating is crisp. The end result will be a greasy mess. You're better off with the green salad.

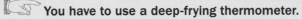 **You have to use a deep-frying thermometer.**

You constantly have to adjust the stove's heat to keep the oil at a constant temperature. If the oil's temperature goes too high, the crust will burn before the food inside is cooked through. You're better off with a green salad.

The pan can't be crowded.

If you dump a whole chicken in a 4-quart saucepan of hot oil, the temperature will drop precipitously and the food will get soggy before the oil comes back up to the right temperature. You're better off with a green salad.

The oil has to have a high smoke point.

You want refined peanut oil, soybean oil, refined canola oil, or olive oil. These oils can be heated to the high point without fear of an explosion. Once they catch fire, you can easily burn down your kitchen. You're better off with a green salad.

The minute the food comes out of a deep fryer, put it on a wire rack so the excess surface oil will drip off. Don't put the fried things on a paper towel–lined plate. That only lets the food sit in its own juices, rendering the crust soggy.

Modern French fries, however, present a distinct problem: they're mostly fried twice—once with a low-temperature oil to cook them through, so they can then sit on the shelf for a while or even be frozen indefinitely, but all the while assuring they pick up tons of excess fat; then again with a high-temperature oil to crunch them up. A really bad frying technique renders them really unhealthy.

In the end, it's not just bad frying that makes things so unhealthy; it's also the food fried—or the batter used: chicken with its skin on, cheese sticks, a rich buttermilk coating, maybe even some egg yolks in that batter. None of these things will break the bank on its own—but add some oil, combine it with slipshod frying, and you may well be in for a perfect storm. Take the skin off the chicken, watch your technique, and save the cheese sticks for another day. But don't malign something so wonderful as fried foods.

MYTH #83

EGGS RAISE YOUR CHOLESTEROL.

YOU ALSO DON'T HAVE TO STUDY FOR A BLOOD TEST.

It's really not all that simple. Eggs do contain dietary cholesterol—and a fair amount. About 212 milligrams per large egg, all of it in the yolk. That puts eggs up there with the other big dietary cholesterol foods: shrimp, duck, and liver.

But dietary cholesterol doesn't peel off the yolk and shellac itself to your arteries. Dietary cholesterol, the kind that comes from animal products, is not the same thing as blood-serum cholesterol. One goes in your mouth; the other ends up in your arteries. In between, there are these things called your digestive track and your liver. They make up a rather effective filtration system, what with the acid breakdown of food, the zillions of microbes eating things up, and the membrane walls between you and what you eat. Draw blood the day after Yom Kippur and it won't smell like lox.

Thus, a study in 2008 at the Harvard Medical School found that otherwise healthy men could eat up to *seven* eggs *per day* and see no increase in their risk for coronary disease.

Despite such good news, dietary cholesterol can still turn up in your arteries as blood-serum cholesterol, even with all that is standing guard. You can swamp any border.

The crux of the matter is found in two little words used in that study: *otherwise healthy.* Genetics do come into play. Between 75 and 85 percent of your serum cholesterol level is endogenous—that is, made by your own body. Blood-serum cholesterol is made by every cell you've got—and primarily by the cells in your liver, which dispense more when your levels do not conform to a genetically determined count. That's why there are star athletes with 3 percent body fat *and* high serum cholesterol numbers, even bad ratios between HDL and LDL cholesterol.

Still, blood-serum cholesterol is not a bad thing. You need it to live. It makes up the bile necessary for the proper digestion of fats; it also wends its way to your sex organs where it's synthesized into all the sex hormones you could ever need. Blood-serum cholesterol is nature's Viagra!

The remaining 15 to 25 percent of your blood-serum cholesterol comes from external sources—that is, from what you eat. For some people, their liver regulates the level, making less when they eat fattier foods. For others, like those who have diabetes or genetic proclivities, their bodies will produce blood-serum cholesterol in vats as they chow down on everything from ice cream to bacon. These people will find that all dietary cholesterol, even that found in eggs, will raise their blood-serum cholesterol levels. When that smaller percent from external sources balloons and comes up against already high cholesterol levels, it can spell trouble. But for most of us, it doesn't.

And keep this in mind, the good news *and* the bad: there's evidence to suggest that moderate, routine exercise over time readjusts the cholesterol levels for the better; and there's evidence to suggest that a diet consistently high in fats and carbs over time readjusts cholesterol levels for the worse.

So have an egg or two once in a while. You'll get lots of vitamin D, necessary for proper calcium absorption, and plenty of protein. Afterward, take the dog for a nice, long walk.

And while we're at it, one more thing: dietary cholesterol comes from animal products. It does not—cannot—come from plants. So the next time you see a piece of dark chocolate or a package of green beans or a carton of orange juice or a box of oat bran that states it's *cholesterol free,* know that the claim is true but utterly disingenuous. Of course, those things don't have cholesterol. They never did and they never will. None was made from an animal product. The real news would be if there *was* a box of oat bran that contained dietary cholesterol. *New bacon-laced oat bran.* Now that'd be a reason to get out of bed in the morning.

DRINKING COFFEE LEADS TO HIGH BLOOD PRESSURE.

NOT ACCORDING TO THE EXPERTS.

An eight-ounce cup of coffee *can* raise your blood pressure temporarily. But not by much—by as little as 3 millimeters of mercury, or in rare cases as much as 14 millimeters of mercury. If your blood pressure measures a perfectly normal 120/70, that increase is marginal; if your numbers are 160/110, it's more frightening. But even a body as austere as the Joint National Committee on Hypertension says that there's no credible link between the disease and coffee intake.

We'd also be remiss not to point this out: if you're in that latter, 160/110 group, things were frightening *before* you drank that cup of joe. The coffee didn't get you to those elevated levels; your genes did. And a host of other factors, like your weight, your salt intake (if you're genetically susceptible), and your stress levels.

Caffeine does jack you up, no doubt about it. But not for long. It's self-limiting. It prods your kidneys, which in turn get rid of it.

Still, some studies suggest *large* amounts of caffeine can block a hormone that keeps your arteries wide. Others have found that caffeine prompts the release of adrenaline, the fight-or-flight response, which causes your blood pressure to rise. But neither of these was enough to get the Joint National Committee on Hypertension concerned.

Apparently your body also gets used to the stuff, which means you can build up a tolerance to it. So much so that one recent study found that 15 percent of the people who drink coffee regularly actually experience a *drop* in blood pressure levels after consuming it, not an elevation.

Thus, if you're still in that 160/110 blood pressure group, you might want to forgo that pot of coffee before running on the treadmill or mowing the lawn. You might also want to see a doctor.

In the end, it's probably all about your genes. You get hypertension from your family. But you already knew that from the last holiday you spent with them, didn't you? Go get yourself a nice shot of espresso and chill out.

SUGAR LEADS TO HYPERACTIVITY.

SEEING IS NOT NECESSARILY BELIEVING.

It's a birthday party. The children are running around like banshees, splashing watercolors on the walls. Some parent inevitably says, "It's the cake."

You think, *Wait a minute. I had a piece of cake. I'm not pulling my dress up over my head.*

But everyone's nodding. So you sort of go with it. Except you shouldn't.

First off, face it: if you corral a bunch of eight-years-olds in a room and feed them nothing but steamed broccoli, all the while plying them with games and toys, knocking balls against the wall and playing hopscotch, singing songs off-key, and otherwise offering constant stimulation, those kids will soon enough turn into banshees. But we'll bet you dollars to donuts you won't blame the steamed broccoli.

In fact, there's never been any credible research evidence to suggest that sugar leads to hyperactivity. In 1994, an article in *The Journal of Abnormal Child Psychology* found that parents who *believe* sugar causes hyperactivity will see it, even in children who ate no sugar at all, although the parents were told they had.

That said, there is a corollary to this myth that is actually true: excessive sugar intake can cause a crash—just as the excessive intake of any carbohydrate can.

But we're talking excessive, combined with no physical activity to offset the carbs. You sit down in front of the TV with that big carton of mint chocolate chip ice cream. You make your way through a healthy hunk of it. Your insulin levels go bonkers, blood rushes to your gut to aid digestion, and you feel really sluggish, all from having slammed back a calorie-dense, poor-nutrition food in very little time while sitting around doing nothing except pressing the buttons on the remote control.

But note that before the sluggishness, you didn't first jump up and run around like a banshee. You just sat there. A crash doesn't necessarily indicate a preceding mania. Except on Wall Street. But that's another story.

FROZEN VEGETABLES ARE LESS NUTRITIOUS THAN FRESH ONES.

LIFE IS ALL ABOUT COMPLEXITY.

Frozen vegetables are most often picked at the peak of ripeness, when they're nutrient rich and dense. By contrast, the ones destined for the fresh produce section were probably picked early so that they'd be durable for transport. The frozen ones gained a better nutritional profile as they sat on the stem, waiting to get picked.

What's more, many of the ones destined to be sold fresh are also going to be artificially ripened with chemicals such as ethylene gas. Even if they aren't, they may—*may*—get a little sweeter as they sit around in the cardboard boxes; mostly, they will just get a little softer. But in any case, they will not be gaining any nutritional value.

In fact, the fresh ones lose some of their nutritional value. A green bean picked and left at room temperature for three days may have only a third as much vitamin C as one picked and flash-frozen.

However, don't jump to quick conclusions. Not all frozen vegetables are created equal. Look for the USDA grade *fancy* on the packaging. These are the best vegetables, the highest in nutrition, usually the ripest and largest of the crop.

Also, buy frozen vegetables without any chemical or fake-flavor folderol. Be wary of any additives or preservatives in frozen vegetables. Be on the lookout for added sodium—as well as so-called *natural flavors,* which can be just a big doping of MSG. And keep in mind that over prolonged storage, months and months, the nutritional value of frozen vegetables can also degrade. Check the date on the package before you buy it.

But here's a plus: you don't need to cook many frozen vegetables. Corn and bell peppers can be thawed and tossed into salads right from the bag. Others don't need to be heated beyond a quick warm-up, probably in the microwave. The blanching, freezing, and thawing process that got them there has already broken down many of the indigestible fibers.

Still and all, when it comes to flavor, nothing beats fresh fruits and vegetables. Flavor is a hallmark of freshness. Fresh almost always wins that game. But when it comes to nutrition, here's the final hierarchy of what's what:

☞ First, a fresh, ripe vegetable at a farmers' market picked within the last 24 hours.

☞ Second, most frozen vegetables without added chemicals.

☞ Finally, most fresh vegetables from the supermarket's produce section.

COOKING VEGETABLES DESTROYS THEIR VITAMIN CONTENT.

NOT ALWAYS, SHERLOCK.

Raw may well mean crunchier. It sometimes means fresher. But raw vegetables are not necessarily better for you. For example:

☞ *Steamed* broccoli contains higher levels of glucosinolate compounds, a terrific antioxidant with cancer-fighting properties.

☞ Steaming, boiling, or roasting carrots breaks down their cellular walls and helps you then consume more carotenoids, the powerful antioxidants that are full of vitamin A.

☞ And you can get more lycopine from cooked tomatoes than from raw ones.

However, in all these cases, other nutrients did degrade—like folic acid and vitamin C. Depending on how long the vegetables were cooked, these may have been lost entirely. Vitamin C is flat-out destroyed by heat. Which is why *pasteurized* orange juice has vitamin C added back into it, a maddening conundrum of the modern world.

Heat, time, and moisture are the key factors in the degradation of nutritional content. Thus, vegetables should be cooked as quickly as possible, at as low a temperature as possible, with as little water as possible—which means boiling is almost always out.

Steaming is a great alternative. Yes, it is a high-temperature method; but it's also really fast, much quicker than boiling. And the nutrients don't dissolve into the water, the very water that's going to go through the colander in the sink and right down the drain.

Soup is a good compromise because although it's a high-liquid environment, you're also going to consume that liquid, with all the dissolved vitamins and minerals in it. Stir-frying is great because it's fast and uses very little moisture, even with the high heat. If you leave the vegetables in larger chunks, you'll have fewer vitamins lost to heat and air.

Roasting? Not so much because of the very long time in the heat. However, roasting does offer the best flavor since the natural sugars have a chance to caramelize. Steamed beets may be better for you but roasted beets taste finer.

In the end, no matter which method you choose, keep those vegetables crisp. Chewing signals the vagus nerve, the one that connects our heads to our guts. Stimulating that nerve is one of the primary ways we then experience satiety. Which is what this whole eating thing is about in the first place, right?

TOMATO VEGETABLE SOUP

Serves 4

Nothing beats vegetable soup. Rich and satisfying, soup retains many of the nutrients in the liquid, so you're drinking your vitamins. And nothing beats the taste of cream. But the secret is not to use too much. It's culinary—and dietary—dynamite and should be used judiciously, just enough to bring real satisfaction to every spoonful. Oh, and make sure to have some crunchy bread on hand for dipping.

1 tablespoon olive oil

1 tablespoon unsalted butter

1 small yellow onion, finely chopped

*2 medium celery ribs, halved lengthwise
    and finely chopped*

*1 medium red bell pepper, cored,
    seeded, and finely chopped*

1 medium carrot, cut into thin rings and finely chopped

*1 medium yellow-fleshed potato,
    peeled and finely chopped*

½ pound green beans, cut into small pieces

2 medium garlic cloves, minced

One 28-ounce can crushed tomatoes with their juice

1 cup reduced-sodium vegetable broth

2 teaspoons dried oregano

2 teaspoons dried thyme

1 teaspoon salt

½ teaspoon freshly ground black pepper

¼ cup heavy or whipping cream

1. Heat the oil and butter in a pot over medium heat. (The oil actually protects the butter from burning for a while so that it doesn't darken so quickly.) Stir in the onion, celery, red bell pepper, carrot, potato, and green beans. Keep stirring over the heat until the onion starts to soften, a couple of minutes. (You can also substitute a 1-pound bag of frozen mixed vegetables for the pepper, carrot, potato, and green beans. No need to thaw it. Just dump it in the pot.) Add the garlic; cook less than 1 minute.

2. Pour in the tomatoes, then the broth. As the liquid comes up to simmer, stir well to make sure everything brown comes off the bottom and sides of the pot.

3. Now stir in the oregano, thyme, salt, and pepper. (The dried herbs can stand up to the intense heat—and because they're going to stew a long time, they'll dump their fragrant oils into the broth as they rehydrate.)

4. Bring the whole thing to a full simmer over medium-high heat, stirring occasionally. Then cover the pot, reduce the heat, and simmer slowly until the vegetables are tender when prodded with a fork, about 1 hour. Stir the soup now and again to make sure nothing's sticking and to make sure the heat's not too high.

5. Stir in the cream, then simmer uncovered for 5 minutes, stirring often. It's ready. If you end up with any leftovers, these can be frozen in individual containers for a quick microwaveable lunch.

RICE AND BEANS TOGETHER PROVIDE THE FULL PROTEIN CHAIN OF MEAT.

THINK AGAIN.

In *Diet for a Small Planet,* the runaway best seller from the '60s, Frances Moore Lappé sang the praises of rice and beans together and crescendoed into a conclusion replete with bureaucrat-speak to make it legit, praising the whole nonsense as *protein complementarity.* It sounded so good that sober bunches like The National Research Council and The American Dietetic Association picked up the refrain and belted it out.

Here's how they all ended up on this false note: beans lack the (alleged) *full complement* of amino acids. Those missing need to be supplemented. They're found in rice. Eat beans and rice together and you get said full complement.

Except it doesn't work that way. Mostly because beans contain *protein-like* amino acids which everyone conveniently calls *incomplete proteins.* Some of these are so simple, they're nutritionally ineffective; others are admittedly terrific nutrients.

Rice does supplement the protein-like aminos—with more protein-like aminos. So you end up with a passel of very weak chains with a few great ones thrown in for good measure. But you never end up with the *full complement*. You'll get that from meat and fish.

And from plants, too. You can indeed get all the protein you need from a vegetarian diet. Start with potatoes; add some broccoli, Brussels sprouts, or asparagus; throw in some mushrooms, okra, or beets; and toss in a handful of nuts (particularly walnuts, Brazil nuts, and pistachios), some seeds (particularly almonds and pumpkin seeds), or lentils. You're ready for a workout—or just a good hard day at work. What's more, your body stores amino acids for future use. So if you're eating a balanced diet, you have them in the bank.

One more thing: although Lappé herself recanted her theory in a revision of her book in 1981, rice and beans are nonetheless a terrific combination, a wonderful go-to dinner when you want to lay off the meat for a while. You should eat them together because they're delicious, particularly with some salsa on top, but not because you're faking yourself out with some nonsense about protein complementarity.

SWEET POTATOES ARE BETTER FOR YOU THAN POTATOES.

SOME BRIGHT IDEAS ARE REALLY JUST BEGINNER'S LUCK.

First off, sweet potatoes aren't potatoes. They're rhizomes, related to ginger and (yes) morning glories. They're the underground stem of a plant, sending out roots and shoots from their kinks and nodes. They prefer lush, humid, almost tropical environments, like South Carolina or Jamaica.

These days, the closest to the original we have is a Caribbean *batata,* a dark red rhizome with cream, pale flesh, starchier than our run-of-the-mill sweet potato and so sugary sweet that it oozes juices even before it's cooked. If you're lucky enough to find one of these babies at a farmers' market or high-end grocery store, snatch it up, get it home, put it on a baking tray, and roast it in a 400°F oven until tender. The tray will have to be soaked for hours to get off the caramelized sugars, but the whole thing will have been worth it, especially if you mix a little butter with a dash of cayenne and some salt, then smear it on top.

Potatoes—such as yellow-fleshed Yukon Golds, little red-jacket potatoes, and even baking potatoes—are tubers. Like big underground seeds, they are microcosms of the plant itself, produced so they can hold over the winter and propagate the species the next year. They prefer cold, harsh climates, like Maine or Idaho—or the high Andes.

The closest to the original we have these days is the purple potato, a descendant from the ones the Spanish conquistadors found in South America and took back to Europe. It made the priests shiver. You see, potatoes came from under the ground—that is, the devil's domicile. Things that grew down there must have nefarious ways. So for years, potatoes were grown in Spain as a curiosity, like Venus flytraps.

In the end, to compare sweet potatoes to potatoes is to compare apples to Brussels sprouts. But if you just want to know which is better for you, well, it depends. We're talking about two different botanical species. The nutritional profiles are completely different.

A sweet potato is very high in vitamin C, has lots of beta-carotene (like carrots), packs plenty of fiber, and is a relatively good source of B_6, copper, and iron. It also contains nightshade alkaloids, found in tomatoes, eggplants, and some other vegetables, which can cause an allergic reaction in some people.

A potato is also very high in vitamin C, has lots of potassium as well as vitamin B_6, is a good source of fiber, and a pretty good source of manganese and even protein.

Both are great vegetables. It's what you do with your rhizome or tuber that matters. The butter, the sour cream, and the cheese. These can make any vegetable "bad for you."

9

OTHER STUFF THE TEXAS BOARD OF EDUCATION HAS PROBABLY APPROVED

Historical Myths

They say history's written by the winners. It's also written by the lazy. They get the facts wrong, slant some, make up others, and finally come out with a tale that sounds plausible but is complete bunkum.

Most of our culinary historical myths are based on just that: the ability to sound plausible. A word is mispronounced or misspelled, a true history is reduced until all of its natural complexity is lost, and then it's all tarted up with a punch line and told endlessly, increasing its plausibility by sheer repetition.

Come to think about it, that's how most myths get started.

So let's set the record straight on a few of the "historical" ones that make their appearance everywhere from grade-school textbooks to prime-time cooking shows.

MARCO POLO INTRODUCED PASTA TO EUROPE FROM CHINA.

FUHGEDDABOUDIT!

Of all the historical culinary myths, the one about Marco Polo's introducing pasta to Italy after lollygagging about Kubla Khan's court may be the most persistent. But consider this timeline:

- 1279 CE. There's a reference to a basket of dried pasta in the catalogue of effects from the estate of a Genoese soldier-gentleman.

- 1295 CE. Marco Polo returns to Venice.

So he didn't *introduce* spaghetti to Italy, but he may well have brought some back with him from the Far East. Or perhaps from one of his stops in the Middle East. Even Arabic cultures lay claim to the origins of the noodle. All of which brings us to the central question: Who invented pasta?

As of this writing, the Chinese. In 2005, archaeologists found remnants of spaghetti-like tangles at the Lajia site on the Yellow River. Carbon-dating pushed the noodles to about 2000 BCE, about the time of the biblical patriarchs. Prior to this find, the earliest known Chinese reference to noodles was in an East Han Dynasty book written between 25 and 225 CE.

However, there's a problem: these noodles were made from ground millet, not wheat. When we say *pasta*, we generally mean *wheat* noodles. And now the Chinese lose the advantage. Wheat is a crop from ancient Turkey, grown somewhere in the wild and woolly Karacadag Mountains since at least 8000 BCE, six thousand years before those mummified Chinese noodles. Wheat spread from this region across the world—by 6500 BCE, to modern Germany; by 6000 BCE, to the Italian peninsula; by 3000 BCE, up to Scandinavia; and by 2000 BCE, at long last, out to China.

What's more, an Etruscan tomb north of Rome from about 400 BCE has a mural of servants mixing flour and water, then shaping it into noodles. Most culinary historians believe that this pasta was baked, not boiled. Still, a miss is as good as a mile. The Italian peninsula can probably lay claim, not to noodles in general, but to our current notion of pasta.

Although not as we currently enjoy it. *Boiling* pasta may well have originated in Arabic cultures, especially since couscous, a product similar to pasta, was already being boiled in Palestine in the second century CE. Islamic geographer Muhammad al-Idrisi mentioned boiled noodles as a prize of civilization a hundred years before Marco Polo got back from the Far East.

So to sum up:

- The Chinese first came up with the notion of noodles.
- The Italians first came up with what we call *pasta*.
- The Arabs first boiled it.

IN THE MIDDLE AGES, THEY USED SPICES OR HONEY TO COVER THE TASTE OF ROTTEN MEAT.

TOO MANY FREAKS, NOT ENOUGH CIRCUSES.

For decades, professors of all things medieval have tried to debunk this myth—which rests on several debatable beliefs:

- that anything not modern is to be feared (thank you, Herr Freud),

- that we're better than anyone who ever lived before us (thank you, Mr. Darwin),

- and that we can somehow override the safeguards in our taste buds and noses (thank you, Travel Channel).

If our medieval progenitors chowed down on spoiled meat, chances are we wouldn't be here. Because our forebears would have died early on. Also, stayed barren. Hang all the tapestries you want, but nothing spoils the mood like 1) the heaves and 2) the runs.

This historical boondoggle got started in J. C. Drummond's *The Englishman's Food: Five Centuries of English Diet,* first published in 1939. Drummond was a rather prominent figure, a scientific adviser to the crown, but apparently given this myth, prone to making it up out of whole cloth. Although his medieval howler has become a staple of gross-out stories about the Middle Ages, we can refute it on three counts.

1. **Drummond's hypothesis was that poor folks bought bad meat and had to shellac it to make it palatable. But even if they could have afforded meat, they most definitely could not have afforded those shellacking spices, the true marker of luxury.**

2. **Even by scrupulous modern standards, medieval cookbooks are full of warnings about rancid meat. Note this bit from *Le Ménagier de Paris*, a housekeeping manual from 1393 CE, translated by Janet Hinson:**

    Note that some hang their pigs in the Easter season and the air yellows them; and it would be better for them to keep them in salt as they do in Picardy, even though the flesh is not so firm, it seems; nevertheless you get better service from bacon which is fair and white than from yellow, because however good the yellow may be, it is too repulsive and causes disgust when viewed.

Yes, some medieval recipes asked cooks to submerge joints and haunches in vats of honey—which is a preservative. It seals moisture and oxygen away from the exposed flesh, keeping it safe for a limited time, until the king wanted his next feast perhaps. Were the meat rotten, it would still smell and taste rotten, honey or not.

3. You've experienced the problem firsthand. You've eaten Chinese takeout. You've wondered about the chicken. You ended up not eating it because it smelled like New York City on an August afternoon. And that chicken was covered with chiles, garlic, spices, you name it. Yet you shied away. And if you didn't, you will next time. Provided there is a next time.

MEDIEVAL LASAGNA

Dinner for 8

No, it's not authentic, but we did adapt it from medieval sources—which used all sorts of chicken parts, some none too savory for today's lasagna lovers. The original was also not baked but stacked up on a plate. Still, it's hard to argue with it as it now stands.

2 tablespoons olive oil
1 tablespoon unsalted butter
1 small yellow onion, minced
1 medium carrot, thinly sliced and minced

3 medium garlic cloves, minced

8 ounces pancetta (that is, unsmoked,
  cured, Italian bacon), diced

1¾ pounds diced, boneless, skinless chicken thighs

½ cup dry white wine or dry vermouth

3 tablespoons minced sage leaves

2 bay leaves

1 tablespoon honey

½ teaspoon grated nutmeg

¼ teaspoon ground cloves

2 cups reduced-sodium, fat-free, canned chicken broth

¼ cup reduced-sodium, canned tomato paste

12 cooked lasagna noodles, rinsed (see page 223)

6 ounces Parmigiano-Reggiano, shaved

6 tablespoons pine nuts, toasted in a
  dry skillet until lightly brown

6 tablespoons chopped golden raisins

6 tablespoons heavy or whipping cream

1. Heat the olive oil and butter in a large saucepan over medium heat. When the butter melts, add the onion, carrot, and garlic. Cook, stirring frequently, until the onion turns translucent, about 3 minutes.

2. Dump in the diced pancetta; continue cooking and stirring over the heat until it's browned and frizzled at its edges, about 4 minutes. Then stir in the diced chicken and cook, stirring often, until it loses its raw, pink color, about 5 minutes.

3. Stir in the wine, sage, bay leaves, honey, nutmeg, and cloves. Cook for 2 minutes, scraping up any browned bits on the pan's bottom; then pour in the broth and tomato paste. (No, there were no tomatoes in medieval

Europe. Recipes such as this one called for stale bread as a thickener. But we couldn't resist the modern twist.) Stir well and bring to a full simmer. Set the lid askew on the pan, reduce the heat to low, and simmer slowly for 1 hour, stirring often and covering the pan completely if the ragù starts to get too dry.

4. Position the rack in the center of the oven and preheat the oven to 375°F. Build the lasagna. Spoon ½ cup ragù into a 9 x 13-inch baking dish. Top with four noodles, overlapping as necessary. Spread a third of the remaining ragù on them, then half the Parmigiano-Reggiano, half the nuts, and half the raisins. Drizzle with half the cream. Lay four more noodles on top. Spread half the remaining sauce on top, then the rest of the cheese, the rest of the nuts, the rest of the raisins, and the rest of the cream. Lay the remaining four noodles on top and cover with the remaining ragù.

5. Cover the baking dish with parchment paper, then seal it with aluminum foil. Bake for 40 minutes. Then uncover the baking dish and continue baking until the top is brown and bubbling, about 10 more minutes. Cool for 5 minutes before cutting into squares to serve.

PUMPERNICKEL WAS SO NAMED BECAUSE NAPOLEON THOUGHT IT WAS FIT FARE FOR HIS HORSE.

SACRÉ BLEU!

The story goes that Napoleon had been away from Paris and its heavenly baguettes for months. It was rainy, bleak, and muddy in Germany. Ahead lay Russia. More rain, more mud. This was no country for really short men.

As Napoleon surveyed his troops, his horse bucked, a warning that someone was approaching. The emperor patted Nichol's neck, looked around. A cook was on his way with a loaf of bread. Rations had been poor. The man bowed and cut off a hunk, about the color of his smeared boots.

The emperor took a bite. It was horrible: coarse and mealy. He spit it out. "C'est pain pour Nichol," he said.

Pain pour Nichol. Painpournichol. Pumpernickle.

We didn't say it wasn't a stretch.

In truth, the word *pumpernickel* was used in Germany for centuries before our height-challenged tyrant arrived on the scene. In 1668, Hans Jakob Christoffel von Grimmelshausen mentioned this bread in his satirical novel, *Der Abenteuerliche Simplicissimus Teutsch,* about the adventures of a benighted young man who survives during the Thirty Years' War by fighting for both sides, along the way suffering the indignities of poor rations and Russia. Apparently it was ever thus in European military service.

Pumpernickel originated in Westphalia, a region in north, central Germany along the Rhine. It's about like Périgord in France: no one's sure exactly where the borders are but everyone's sure the place exists, mostly because of how much blood has been spilled there. Westphalia was one of the central battlegrounds of our benighted young man's war, in actuality one of the world's more awful conflicts, one that wiped out almost a third of central Europe. The final treaty is now called The Treaty of Westphalia, although the parties at the time actually referred to it as The Treaty of Exhaustion, if that tells you anything.

It's understandable that von Grimmelshausen would feature this heavy, coarse bread in his fictional account of the war's toll. Pumpernickel is a dark, chewy, whole-grain, rye bread. It's meant both to stave off hunger and move the bowels. It's unlikely that a diminutive emperor from Corsica who spent years developing a snooty Parisian palate to hide his rural roots would ever have had occasion to eat it.

And by the way, Julius Caesar didn't invent the Caesar salad either.

GERMAN CHOCOLATE CAKE COMES FROM GERMANY.

NEIN, DANKE.

This is the "Who's on First?" of culinary mythology. An Englishman by the name of Samuel German, who had nothing to do with inventing the delicious layer cake that bears his name, did however invent the chocolate.

Sam, who was something at a whiz with the confection, had come to the United States to make his fortune. While working for the Baker's Chocolate Company in Dorchester, Massachusetts, he came up with the formula for a sweet baking variety around 1852. Most folks didn't like the bitter stuff that passed off as chocolate in those days. So Sam added more sugar to the mix, ever a selling point in the United States.

His formulation gave Baker's brand a necessary oomph. His chocolate bars spread as far as California during the Gold Rush, a luxury treat in exchange for hard-won nuggets. Sam, too, got a little treat for his efforts. The company put his name on the package: *Baker's German's Sweet Chocolate.* No telling if he got any profit-sharing.

Things went along fine until 1957. Sam was long gone, of course. Newspaper food sections were a new concept, a way to make the paper a must-have for homemakers, not just their husbands. Unfortunately, the editorial staff for these food sections was about as sparse as it is now. They relied on readers to send in recipes.

And they did. In basketfuls. One industrious Dallas, Texas, housewife sent in one to her local paper for a moist, sky-high layer cake, made with buttermilk and her favorite sweet chocolate. She probably didn't come up with the recipe herself—there were plenty of recipes for buttermilk chocolate cakes in those days—but she did name it for her brand of choice: *German's Chocolate Cake.*

By then, General Foods owned Baker's Chocolate. The company was suddenly selling out of its *Baker's German's Sweet Chocolate.* They couldn't figure out why. A plucky researcher traced the trend back to that Dallas newspaper.

Sensing a craze, the company grabbed the recipe. Always on the lookout for brand extensions, they reformulated it a bit, using another one of their products: sweetened flaked coconut.

General Foods then flashed their revamped version around the country to every paper they could find. The recipe became an American sensation long before Twitter: *German's Chocolate Cake.* Eventually, that *apostrophe-s* proved too difficult to say and everyone just called it *German Chocolate Cake.* But take a minute and say it right: German's Chocolate Cake. Give Sam his due.

10

PSSST, I THINK MY TOASTER IS WATCHING ME

Myths About Kitchen Gadgetry

The twenty-first century is proving to be a time when technology changed *personal* life dramatically and lastingly. By contrast, in the twentieth century, its change was experienced more on a macro level. The big technological inventions back then changed the ways families went about their lives.

Nowhere more so than in the kitchen. The range and scope of the change from 1900 to 1999 is dramatic: from wood fires to gas stoves, from lye and lukewarm water to dishwashers, from all-day food preparation to dinner in minutes.

Naturally, some of that change brought with it free-floating anxieties, as change often will. Even today, in almost every cooking class we teach, we run into people who express a fear of the kitchen. When asked to visualize that fear, they inevitably point to an appliance or gadget: "my stove," "my refrigerator," "those knives." In a recent cooking class, one woman actually singled out her baking sheets.

Let's take the bubble of that boil. Sure, cooking is work. Messy, too. But it's been greatly simplified by technological innovations, so it doesn't need to be made complex again by a bunch of myths.

GAS IS BETTER THAN ELECTRIC.

WHO SAYS?

Yes, chefs cook with gas. But they're no judges. Their burners are on high all the time. Many of the advantages of gas are lost in their kitchens.

And the difference between gas and electric stoves is not one of economics. According to the American Council for an Energy Efficient Economy, there's little cost or energy savings between them.

Still, there are positives and negatives to both.

GAS

 1. Control.

It used to be that gas was better in terms of the speed with which it could deliver high heat—and also drop that heat back down to low. These days, electric induction burners heat up just as fast as gas, so some of that advantage has been nixed. However, you can still pull a gas flame *down* in a second with very little residual heat. Thus, gas offers you better control when you're lowering the heat. You don't have to wait for the coil to cool down. Things don't scorch as easily—so long as they're watched.

2. Visual monitoring.

You can see a gas flame. You know it's on—and you know how high it's on. With an electric stove, you don't know what you've got because the pot covers the burner. You have to rely on the gauge. Which isn't always reliable.

 ### 3. Kitchen choreography.

You can lift a pot off a gas flame to stir into the corners or toss ingredients in a tilted skillet—and you still have heat, rising from the flame. With an electric stove, you lose a lot of the heat when you break contact with the burner.

 ### 4. Durability.

Gas stoves don't crack the way glass cooktops can.

 ### 5. The primeval factor.

Here's the real reason people like gas: they can cook over a fire. And indoors, to boot.

ELECTRIC

 ### 1. Simmering.

By and large, electric stoves can simmer at lower temperatures than gas stoves. You can get the heat low enough to count the bubbles as they form. Since this is the preferred method for braising, long-cooked stews and such are better on electric ranges.

2. No escaping heat.

Modern electric stoves bring water to a boil more quickly than gas ranges: more of the heat goes directly into the pot (which covers the burner completely). A gas stove heats up your kitchen because some of the flame misses the pot and disperses.

 ## 3. Less temperamental.

Gas burners need frequent calibration. The gas jets also get clogged. They need constant cleaning.

 ## 4. You can't blow up your house.

Electric's got that going for it, too, which is nice.

In the end, spend your money on high-quality pots, pans, and skillets. They can make up for a less-efficient range, but a great range cannot make up for shoddy cookware.

PLASTIC CUTTING BOARDS ARE MORE HYGIENIC THAN WOODEN ONES.

RUBBISH!

Yes, at the very moment you unwrap them from their sealed factory packaging, the plastic cutting board may be slightly more hygienic than the wooden one. Plop a chicken breast onto either and you remove any advantages. But don't worry. Both can still be washed and disinfected. Use a diluted chlorine bleach solution (1 teaspoon bleach for every quart of water) or a diluted vinegar solution (1 part white vinegar to 5 parts water). Pour the solution over both sides of the board, let it stand in the sink for a couple of minutes, rinse well, and pat dry with clean paper towels. You're back on a level playing field.

Until you actually cut on a cutting board. Now the game tips in favor of the wooden one.

Wood is the graveyard of food-borne bacteria. Most get absorbed into the fibers of the grain—where they don't just go dormant; they actually pass on to the great cesspool in the sky because of chemical interactions with the wood itself. After much use, a wooden cutting board will show few if—and usually, no—signs of surface contamination.

But a plastic cutting board? It's full of microscopic cracks and grooves. These begin to collect bacteria. Over months of cutting, chopping, and mincing, the plastic gets further scarred with gashes and grooves. It becomes a holding tank. And the bacteria don't die. They go dormant, waiting for something to eat. Like a chicken breast. Or a head of lettuce. Or just about anything *you* want to eat.

That's not to say that the wooden cutting board is fail-safe. If the bacteria have been absorbed and the wood is then scored before they've gone bye-bye, some of the bad pests may return to the surface to contaminate food.

Which is why you need to disinfect a wooden cutting board after each use—so the surface bacteria are destroyed. Every reason to buy wood is negated if you don't clean it.

And there's one more selling point for wood: it's by nature softer than plastic and so easier on your knives. (Glass, by the way, is very hygienic but murder on knives.)

Here are the basic rules of cutting board care:

- Have separate wooden cutting boards for meat and vegetables.
- Discard any cutting boards with deep gashes or grooves, particularly where the wood has split at the seams and formed cracks that can be filled with gunk.
- Buy new cutting boards every now and then, maybe once a year if you do a lot of cooking, maybe every couple of years if you do little.

THE SECRET TO BREWING COFFEE IS TO START WITH COLD WATER.

SOMEBODY WAS UP ALL NIGHT WORKING ON THAT ONE.

Coffee really brings out the snobbery in some people. We once knew someone who only ground his beans by hand; he said the heat of a countertop grinder changed the roast. Among such fussy coffee aficionados we can also find the cold-water devotees—who apparently believe the laws of physics don't apply to them.

When they pour water into their coffeepots, it's heated and showered onto the grounds, or forced through the steam mechanism to make espresso, or slowly percolated up through the tube in that old, electric, countertop behemoth their grandmother used to use. No matter the temperature of the water that goes into the pot, the machine still heats it to a prescribed temperature (between 195°F and 215°F, depending on the model). Cold water simply takes longer to heat. But it does get heated to the preset temperature before it souses the grounds, no matter if it started out cold or hot.

However, there is something to be said for this cold-water fussiness. Hot tap water is (for lack of a better word) processed water. It comes into your water heater from outside your home, gets warmed up in the tank, comes up the pipes where its residual heat can dissolve crusted-on gunk, and finally goes into your coffeemaker.

Cold water is often purer than hot water. It skips the water heater, doesn't dissolve crud as easily. If you're a supertaster, someone who can pinpoint which bed an oyster came from and which specific varietal bean made the chocolate you're enjoying, perhaps you'll notice that small amount of dissolved minerals from your pipes.

If you're really concerned, there are cold-steeping coffee systems, such as the Toddy coffeemaker, a cistern that holds grounds and cold water for twelve hours or so before filtering it through a fabric disk. You store the concentrate in the fridge for weeks on end, adding it to your cup and pouring in boiling water. By the way, the concentrate contains less acid and a good bit less caffeine (only a third of a brewed cup of coffee).

However, in our experience, you'll never have a satisfying cup of hot coffee from these concentrates because you pour it cold into a cup and then add hot water, resulting in lukewarm coffee. For iced coffee, a cold-water filtration system is pretty sweet. But for hot coffee, keep it old school.

MICROWAVE COOKING DESTROYS ESSENTIAL NUTRIENTS.

DEAD WRONG.

Did you know they were once called *radar ranges*? The name was a holdover from bygone days. The first microwave tubes were installed in British radars during World War II. Those tubes, which later morphed into the basis of these ubiquitous, countertop ovens, somehow took on the name of the original radar equipment. The name was later changed because of Cold War politics—at the time, *radar* sounded scary but *microwave* sounded modern and advanced. Go figure.

The microwave oven does work by radiation. However, light from the sun and even heat from a campfire *work by* radiation—although different kinds. Microwave ovens work by electromagnetic radiation. In the case of our countertop ovens, we're talking about nonionizing radiation. In other words, it's not the kind from nuclear bombs or reactors.

All cooking nixes some nutrients and enhances others. Throw a chicken in a hot oven, wait awhile, and you've destroyed a handful of nutrients. You've also made others more accessible to your body. And you've got a nice dinner on the table. It's a trade-off.

There are three factors for destroying essential nutrients in food: time, temperature, and the volume of liquid used. Since a microwave oven cooks more quickly and generally without copious amounts of liquid, fewer nutrients are destroyed than in a conventional oven.

If you're concerned about the nutrient value of cooked food, there are ways to mitigate those key factors we've identified:

- Turn up the oven heat for roasting so that it happens more quickly.

- Use less liquid than you used to.

- Forgo any boiling plans you might have had.

- And use your microwave once in a while. Alice Waters may not approve. But you're not inviting her to dinner anytime soon anyway.

A ROAD MAP FOR MICROWAVE MASHED POTATOES

4 mounds

You can make the best mashed potatoes in the microwave. As a bonus, you don't boil the spuds, so more of their essential nutrients stay intact.

1. You'll need a large, microwave-safe bowl. We've found that the best are the sturdy plastic ones with the lids that have a small vent in the center or to one side. Start with 4 medium Russet or baking potatoes or 8 medium-size yellow-fleshed potatoes. The Russets will be starchier; the yellow-fleshed ones like Yukon Golds, a little denser but perhaps creamier. Wash the potatoes, but do not dry them. And one more thing: you'll note we didn't say to poke them with a fork. Absolutely not! That skin is going to hold in the steam and allow them to cook evenly.

2. Set the potatoes in the bowl, seal the lid, and open the vent. If you don't have one of these fancy bowls, you can use a regular glass bowl and cover it tightly with plastic wrap and make one small slit with a knife in the center.

3. Microwave on high for 8 minutes. Use a hot pad to hold the steamy bowl as you check the potatoes. They should be soft. If not—and the Russets could still be a little firm—put the lid back in place, keep the vent open, and microwave on high for another 2 minutes.

4. Again, watch that steam. It's very hot. Remove the bowl from the microwave and take off the lid (or the plastic wrap, if you used it). You're ready to mash the potatoes. We like using an old-fashioned potato masher because we like a little more texture to the spuds; not quite as creamy. But an electric mixer at medium speed will work as well. Of course, most people add milk (or cream), a little butter, salt, and pepper; then mash or beat at low speed until pretty creamy. But you can add anything to mashed potatoes: canned chicken broth,

Dijon mustard, salt, and pepper; sour cream and chives; broth, yogurt, and a little jarred chutney; minced herbs with the salt and pepper—the sky's really the limit.

Note: We've left the skins on in this recipe since we like the texture they give to mashed potatoes. If you don't want them, you'll need to peel the potatoes after they've cooked in the microwave—and cooled down enough that you can handle them, maybe 20 minutes. Mash them as directed, then reheat the bowlful in the microwave just before you're ready to eat.

MICROWAVES COOK FROM THE INSIDE OUT.

NOT ON THIS PLANE OF REALITY.

Microwave ovens cook by causing molecules to vibrate, usually along the exterior planes, at most an inch or so inside the piece of food. Molecules that make up any liquid are particularly quick to pick up the rhythm. Water, even more so.

These molecules rub up against one another—and against other molecules in the food. Where there's friction, there's heat. Some of the heat generated gets transferred farther inside the food. Meanwhile, more friction, more heat. And so on. The higher the wattage of your microwave, the more friction and the faster food will cook.

As food heats up deep inside, it can develop hot spots. What's more, the temperature of liquids can rise above their natural boiling points. The vibrating friction creates few nucleation sites which would normally allow the formation of steam bubbles (and thus a boil).

Remember how water was particularly prone to the vibration? You can actually heat it beyond its boiling point in a microwave. With few nucleation spots, the vibrating molecules don't jump up to the next level, the boil. They just continue to vibrate madly.

The minute one of these nucleation sites form, it instantly expands with steam—and pops. When you stick a spoon into a microwave-hot cup of tea, or pour in a little sugar, you've introduced lots of minuscule air pockets that quickly offer space, expand, and burst. Thus, your brew explodes out of the cup. Let that cup settle for several seconds before you do anything to it, to let the liquid inside come back down off the detonation point. Or leave a wooden spoon in the cup as it heats in the microwave. The spoon will give the water an easy way to break its vibrating tension and come to a bubble under more normal conditions.

For something like butter, which has water trapped in suspension between fat molecules, heat it in five- to seven-second increments, allowing it to cool in between, thereby taking the bead off the bubble of the hot spots.

In any event, treat everything that comes out of a microwave the same way you'd treat it if it came out of the oven. It's hot. It can burn you. Because a microwave is an oven.

ALUMINUM COOKWARE CAUSES ALZHEIMER'S.

YOU NEED TO REINTERPRET THE DATA.

The link between this metal and the disease rests on three things that have all been refuted:

1. Some early studies found that people with the plaques and tangles associated with Alzheimer's also had higher levels of aluminum. But those levels of aluminum have now been shown to be a product of the disease, not the cause of it.

2. People who are on dialysis often have impaired kidney functions and do not flush aluminum out of their bodies. They soon develop what's known as *dialysis dementia*— which is sort of like Alzheimer's, except it's temporary and a result of kidney failure, not brain failure. When good kidney functioning is restored through proper dialysis, patients gain back much if not all of their mental faculties. In fact, after years of repeated exposure to high levels of aluminum because of failing kidneys, most patients do not develop Alzheimer's.

3. One of the major drugs for Alzheimer's does indeed remove aluminum from the body. But its removal is actually a side effect of the drug, which is designed to affect iron stores. These may have more to do with the disease than first thought.

In people with functioning kidneys, the digestive track filters out most of the aluminum they ingest. Over 99 percent of the stuff just flushes out and down the toilet. And there's a lot to get rid of. It's the third largest factor in the earth's mass, after oxygen and then silicon. (Or silicon and then oxygen, if you live in L.A.) Aluminum is in toothpaste. And antacids. And buffered aspirin. And a host of food additives, mostly as a preservative of some sort. And many vaccines, again as a preservative. And in drinking water: most municipalities use aluminum sulfates to treat public water.

The real reason you don't want aluminum cookware is because aluminum is a soft metal. It scratches and pits. Acidic foods will cause it to flake. You'll end up with thinner pots. And uneven cooking. And unattractive cookware. And bits of metal in your food. Which is why anodized aluminum cookware has proved popular. You get all the conductivity of aluminum without the reactive issues of raw aluminum. But in any event, your cookware probably won't send you to a nursing home. Your kids will.

AN OPEN BOX OF BAKING SODA IN THE FRIDGE ABSORBS ODORS.

YOU'RE BARKING UP THE WRONG TREE.

First off, what in the world are you putting in your fridge that's stinking it up so badly? If you've got two-week-old, used-to-be-raw-but-now-mostly liquid chicken breasts in your hydrator, you need a life coach, not baking soda.

Still, the mere notion of getting rid of that fridge stink has sold a lot of boxes in North America. A brilliant advertising campaign in the early '70s started the whole hullabaloo. Sales of Arm & Hammer baking soda jumped 72 percent in three years. But does the stuff really do any good? Only marginally. If at all.

Baking soda is an alkali—in other words, a substance with a ph of 8 or higher. It interacts with acids—in other words, substances with a ph of 6 or lower. Put a glass with a little acidic vinegar in the sink and stir in a little alkali like baking soda. You'll see what we mean.

Most of the bad smells in your fridge come from decomposing fats. Fats are acidic—and so are many of the stinky molecules that come from them.

If some fat-based stink was floating around inside your fridge, it might come into surface contact with that box of baking soda and might be neutralized at a slow and irregular rate. Problem is, that box is pretty small. What's the chance of a stinky molecule hitting it?

You obviously needed more surface area exposed to have bettered your odds. You could have tried spreading the baking soda on a plate. A really big plate. One that would take up a whole shelf of the fridge. Except that wouldn't even solve the problem. The baking soda crusts when damp. And your fridge is a humid place. So all that water vapor firms up the top of the baking soda. Which means that it can no longer interact with any acid-based stinks that happens to waft by.

And then there's the reaction itself. If the acidic molecules make contact with the baking soda, the attendant reaction will result in an acid salt and (yes) water—which makes the baking soda crust up more and work less. It's a rather self-defeating proposition.

Besides, baking soda is a weak alkali with a ph of around 9. Since this whole neutralizing-by-chance thing will work with any alkali, you'd be better off using a more powerful one. Like Drano. It's got a ph up near 13. Fill a big container with the stuff and put it in your fridge. Take care not to spill any. Now wait. Note that you're not picking up any fridge stink. It may well also be because you're dead from the fumes. But your heirs and assigns will have a marginally better-smelling fridge.

Or you could just find out what's stinking up your fridge and throw it out.

MYTH #101

WHEN YOU'RE MAKING MUFFINS AND YOU HAVE LESS BATTER THAN INDENTATIONS IN THE TIN, FILL THOSE REMAINING INDENTATIONS WITH WATER FOR EVEN BAKING.

NOTHING IS CERTAIN BUT DEATH AND TEXAS— UM, TAXES.

One last myth before we go. And this one's pretty persistent. There are several reasons cookbook authors insist on it:

☞ *1. It keeps your muffin tin from warping.*

Warping? Are you using your great-grandmother's muffin tin? You should be way more worried about tin poisoning than about warping a piece of inexpensive cookware. Today's muffin tins are designed to take the heat. Plus, more and more people use those silicone muffin pans. They don't warp. They bend. Naturally. And heat evenly.

☞ 2. It keeps your muffin tin from smoking.

Residual oils or crusty crud on the pan smoke. Water in the indentations will do nothing to solve that. Get a better dishwasher. Or get a divorce and marry a better dishwasher.

☞ 3. It helps keep your muffin tin from darkening or getting scorched.

First off, how hot is your oven? You shouldn't smelt your muffins. And second, any added water will do nothing for the real reason a muffin pan scorches. Just clean the leftover oils and crud off the thing.

☞ 4. It provides a better crust and higher muffins.

This one actually has a kernel of truth in it. First off, a little steam allows baked goods to have a crunchier crust because surface sugars are dissolved in the moist atmosphere. As they then dry out, they caramelize, creating a crunchier top. And who doesn't want a crunchier top? Second, that humidity allows the batter to rise completely because it keeps the top from hardening before the muffins have fully elevated.

Here's the deal: you want that steam in the oven from the minute the muffins are put inside. Since added water in those indentations will need time to heat up and create steam, it will never do the muffins much good. Besides, you want a dry oven for the last fifteen minutes or so of baking so the tops get crunchy. By the time the added water in the pan starts to steam, you want the oven dry.

If you really want to go all out with this steam trick, heat your oven to the required temperature, then throw an ice cube or two onto the oven's floor. Close the oven door, wait a minute, then open it, get a facial sauna, and slip the filled muffin pan inside onto the rack.

However, this trick will cause the floor of your oven to warp over time. And water can put out the flame in a gas oven and cause the house to go up in flames. A good muffin tin is a much cheaper prospect than a new stove, not to mention a new house.

MARMALADE MUFFINS

About 6 muffins

Here's a riddler: there is no standard muffin tin size. Most of the "large" ones are made with indentations that hold $2/3$ to $3/4$ cup. But there's much variation even in standard sizes. With muffins, all timings are mere guesses, given the difference in the depth of the indentations. You could even use this batter in a mini muffin tin, but then the muffins would bake less than 10 minutes. In any event, fill the indentations three-quarters full, no matter their size.

1¼ cups all-purpose flour
1 teaspoon baking soda
½ teaspoon baking powder

¼ *teaspoon salt*

½ *cup buttermilk, regular or low fat*

6 *tablespoons sugar*

¼ *cup orange marmalade (if there are large strips*
   of orange in it, they'll need to be minced)

1 *teaspoon finely grated orange zest*

1 *large egg, at room temperature*

3 *tablespoons unsalted butter, melted and cooled,*
   plus more for greasing the muffin tin

1½ *tablespoons orange juice*

1. Position the rack in the center of the oven and preheat the oven to 400°F. Coat six indentations of a "standard" muffin tin with butter smeared on a crumpled paper towel. You can also use a silicone muffin tin but you'll need to set it on a baking sheet in the oven so that it rests on a flat surface. (You'll still need to grease the indentations.)

2. Use a whisk or a fork to mix the flour, baking soda, baking powder, and salt in a large bowl.

3. Whisk the buttermilk, sugar, marmalade, and orange zest in a second bowl. There's really no need for an electric mixer here—but a good forearm workout is called for! Give it a real go until smooth.

4. Whisk in the egg, melted butter, and orange juice, again until smooth.

5. Pour the buttermilk mixture into the flour mixture. Use a wooden spoon to stir them together, just until there are no pockets of undissolved flour in the bowl.

6. Spoon the batter into the prepared muffin-tin indentations, filling them three-quarters full. Bake until the tops are rounded and even perhaps a little cracked, until a toothpick into the center of one comes out clean, about 20 minutes. Cool the muffins in their tin on a wire rack for 20 minutes, then turn them out onto the rack and cool completely, about an hour. Store them in a zip-closed plastic bag or sealable container at room temperature for a couple of days or in a similar bag or container in the freezer for a few months, thawing them overnight before enjoying them the next morning.

AT LONG LAST ...

After knocking down 101 myths, we still can't go gallivanting about the food world. Nothing we've said gives us a reason to eat more fat—or less. Nothing gives us a reason to eat more meat—or less. Nothing here gives us a reason to cook one way or the other.

There are no easy answers. In most cases, these weren't outright myths, Zeus on a mountain or Apollo in his chariot, both pretty easily knocked down. Most of these 101 doozies were monochromatic overstatements. They missed the finer nuances in life.

So at the end of it all, let's agree to be more nuanced. Because that's the point: not to be right, but to be faceted and varied, to be open, to know that we all get it wrong—at cooking, sure; but also at love, at truth, at family, at friends, at life. If we're lucky, we stand back up with the deeper knowledge that nobody gets out alive and everybody needs to take a deep breath while they can.

The world needs more forgiveness and grace. And it needs people willing to laugh. There's that old story in the Bible about Abraham and Sarah, without children for so many years it was beyond hopeless. God dropped by one afternoon to have coffee with Abraham and told him not to worry—a child would be along shortly.

Eavesdropping in the tent's drapery, Sarah laughed out loud, giving herself away.

Theologians, rabbis, and ministers have mostly thought it was a laugh of doubt. But maybe it was a laugh of pure joy. She'd just heard the truth, which is the best joke she could have imagined: that life comes back with shocking abandon. That nothing's set in stone. That things work out, not always, but often, and in ways nobody could ever imagine.

Fear not the ones who get it wrong but the ones who think they get it right every time. They miss out on the laughter.

ACKNOWLEDGMENTS

Many thanks to:

Trish Boczkowski, for helping bring yet another beast to bay;

Kate Dresser, for making sure the bay was well-ordered;

Kristin Dwyer, for making sure everyone hears us hounds;

Charlie Corts, Kevin Meyers, and Caitlin Hayes, for videotaping the spoils;

Susan Ginsburg, for organizing our nineteenth chase;

Melanie Tenant at All-Clad Metalcrafters, for equipping the hunt (with pots big enough to boil the title characters);

Harriet Bell, for pointing out other quarry;

And all the people who've ever asked us why their cookies are so flat.

RECIPE INDEX